Trust on the Edge

The New Front Line in IoT Cybersecurity

A C-Suite Guide

By *Bill Lattin* & *David Sequino*

Trust On The Edge

Trust on the Edge: The New Front Line in IoT Cybersecurity

The information contained in this book is provided for educational and informational purposes only. References to specific products, services, or organizations do not constitute endorsement or recommendation unless explicitly stated.

First Edition

Printed in USA

Foreword: The Challenge of Cybersecurity

How did I end up working in the fields of applied cryptography and embedded systems cybersecurity? One of my earliest inspirations came before I even began my career. While in college, I watched a television reporter poke fun at a Yosemite National Park ranger who had received a federal grant to build a more bear-resistant trash container. The reporter mocked the project as frivolous government spending, but the ranger offered a thoughtful rebuttal: it was a difficult problem because between the smartest bears and the dumbest people, there is a surprisingly large overlap in intelligence.

Cryptography and cybersecurity are, at their core, exercises in intelligence. They pit attackers against defenders, with human creativity at the center of the contest. The challenge for all of us working in this field is to design secure systems that account not only for brilliant adversaries, but also for the unintended actions of well-meaning users. The strongest implementations are those that withstand both.

This challenge led me to a lifetime of work helping companies across a wide range of industries design and produce secure products from the ground up.
—Bill Lattin

Table of Contents

Acronyms & Abbreviations

AES — Advanced Encryption Standard
AI — Artificial Intelligence
APT — Advanced Persistent Threat
BI — Business Interruption
CA — Certificate Authority
CAN — Controller Area Network
CI/CD — Continuous Integration / Continuous Deployment
CLM — Certificate Lifecycle Management
CMAC — Cipher-based Message Authentication Code
COGS — Cost of Goods Sold
CVE — Common Vulnerabilities and Exposures
DES — Data Encryption Standard
DSA — Digital Signature Algorithm
ECC — Elliptic Curve Cryptography
ECU — Electronic Control Unit
HMAC — Hash-based Message Authentication Code
HSM — Hardware Security Module
IC — Integrated Circuit
ICS — Industrial Control System
IDS — Intrusion Detection System
IPS — Intrusion Prevention System
IETF — Internet Engineering Task Force
IoT — Internet of Things
ISO — International Organization for Standardization
MAC — Message Authentication Code
MES — Manufacturing Execution System
MFA — Multi-Factor Authentication
NIST — National Institute of Standards and Technology
OT — Operational Technology
OTA — Over-the-Air
PCB — Printed Circuit Board

PLC — Programmable Logic Controller
PKI — Public Key Infrastructure
PQC — Post-Quantum Cryptography
RSA — Rivest–Shamir–Adleman
SAS — Security Architecture Specification
SBOM — Software Bill of Materials
SCADA — Supervisory Control and Data Acquisition
SCM — Software Configuration Management
SHA — Secure Hash Algorithm
SHE — Secure Hardware Extension
SIEM — Security Information and Event Management
SOC — System on Chip
TARA — Threat and Risk Assessment
TRNG — True Random Number Generator
TOE — Target of Evaluation
TLS — Transport Layer Security
TPM — Trusted Platform Module

Our Intent with This Book

When someone mentions cybersecurity, most people immediately think of enterprise cybersecurity, multi-factor authentication, firewalls, intrusion detection systems, VPNs, and similar controls. This perspective overlooks where most CPUs are actually deployed: in the countless small, intelligent devices that are interconnected with one another and with enterprise systems to provide data, control, and services.

Consider mobile phones, modern vehicles, white goods such as refrigerators and washing machines, home security systems, medical devices, avionics, and industrial control systems. These are some of the devices which collectively form the Internet of Things (IoT), and they represent a significant target for attack and misuse. These attack vectors are not limited to the IoT devices themselves. Increasingly, adversaries exploit IoT devices as entry points into enterprise environments through their connections to corporate IT infrastructure. In addition, compromised IoT devices can be marshaled into massive botnets capable of executing denial-of-service attacks against other systems. An attack on one device can therefore enable attacks on many. The cybersecurity front line has expanded.

We are entering a new era in which trust in embedded systems will directly influence national security, economic resilience, and public safety. Artificial intelligence, IoT proliferation, and post-quantum computing threats are converging. If your company manufactures embedded or IoT products, you are a target — either you, your customers, or both are likely to be attacked. Threat actors may include disgruntled employees, organized criminal groups, and nation-states.

Before dismissing the idea of nation-state attacks, consider whether your devices, such as routers, roadside signage, solar inverters, or industrial control systems, are used in critical infrastructure, including water treatment plants, power generation facilities, chemical plants, air traffic systems, or communications backbones. If they are, or if they can be leveraged to cause widespread disruption, they are likely targets. Recent campaigns such as those by China's *Salt Typhoon* and *Volt Typhoon* illustrate this reality.

There are countless books on enterprise cybersecurity. **This is not one of them.** This book distills the authors' combined 60+ years of experience in cryptography and embedded systems cybersecurity to address the unique challenges facing embedded and IoT products and services. It describes the steps required to protect them <u>across their entire lifecycle</u>. Product cybersecurity can only be achieved by defining appropriate architectures, implementations, and controls from design through manufacturing, deployment, operation, and end-of-life. Simply applying enterprise cybersecurity practices to IoT devices is insufficient.

The goal of this book is to provide a high-level, practical guide for C-suite executives and senior management to help you:

1. Understand and articulate the importance of securing IoT products and services against known and emerging threats;
2. Effectively guide your teams in developing a comprehensive cybersecurity strategy that spans the full product lifecycle, from development and manufacturing to operation and end-of-life; and
3. Oversee the consistent and effective implementation of that strategy across all environments involved in the product lifecycle.

Our Intent with This Book

Ultimately, this is a book about trust. Trust that your products will operate reliably in the field and withstand attack. Trust that their supporting services will remain available. Trust that they will not increase your liability exposure. Trust that they will sustain long-term revenue. And trust that your trade secrets and intellectual property will remain protected.

Why You Should Care

The Internet of Things (IoT) encompasses connected products that affect both consumers and enterprises, from autonomous vehicles to the industrial control platforms that underpin modern manufacturing. Of particular concern are safety-critical and life-safety products, where cybersecurity failures can have real-world consequences.

You do not want your product to become a launch pad for attackers targeting your systems or those of your customers. In the consumer space, retail routers and other low-end devices are frequently hijacked to conduct denial-of-service attacks against third-party infrastructure. More than a decade ago, early digital picture frames were shipped with malware embedded in their firmware; when users connected them to their PCs to upload photos, their computers were infected, much to their frustration. This problem still persists. As recently reported by the firm Quokka, Android-based Uhale photo frames were found downloading malicious payloads from China-based servers during boot.

The risks are not limited to inconvenience or reputational harm. Former U.S. Vice President Dick Cheney famously had the remote programming features of his pacemaker disabled due to concerns they could be misused, potentially to kill him. What if this were your product? It is not the publicity you want, nor the product liability you want to assume.

Now consider the enterprise impact. Imagine an automated machining center or 3D printing service processing corrupted files and producing millions of dollars' worth of unusable output. Imagine a semiconductor fabrication facility whose processes are altered, resulting in the loss of high-value silicon wafers. Or consider a chemical refinery whose control systems are compromised, leading to massive product losses or hazardous chemical releases, events for which you may be liable not only for cleanup costs, but also for the long-term health consequences affecting surrounding communities.

Too extreme to imagine? Impossible for your products? The automotive industry once believed this. Initially, manufacturers argued that vehicles could not be attacked. Then they claimed attacks required physical access to individual cars. In 2015, security researchers Charlie Miller and Chris Valasek demonstrated otherwise by remotely compromising an entire class of vehicles, the Chrysler Jeep Cherokee. That attack was conducted by researchers acting responsibly. The industry finally acknowledged the risk and began to take vehicle cybersecurity seriously. How would your organization respond?

Like installing a home alarm after a burglary, many companies ignore IoT cybersecurity until after damage has been done. It does not have to be this way. Cybersecurity does not need to be a cost center; when implemented correctly, it can enhance profitability by enabling capabilities such as secure remote maintenance and feature-based upselling. Tesla demonstrated this by combining secure remote diagnostics with over-the-air (OTA) firmware and feature updates. Want enhanced driving capabilities? Enter a credit card, and the feature is unlocked. That is revenue flowing directly to the bottom line, enabled by cybersecurity.

Cryptography can even make an entire business possible, as illustrated by co-author David Sequino:

In 2002, we designed the first security system for SiriusXM because one of their major investors imposed a hard requirement: funding would only be provided if SiriusXM could prove there would be no revenue leakage. That meant securing satellite broadcasts so only authorized, paying subscribers could decrypt and access content.

We built a Conditional Access System that not only encrypted content but enforced access control at the device level. Each receiver could be uniquely identified, securely provisioned, and revoked if necessary. It was not just about encryption, it was about lifecycle control of authorization across millions of low-cost embedded devices. SiriusXM received their funding.

This experience was transformative. It demonstrated how trust policies could be enforced at scale by binding device identity to capability, and how business logic could be enforced cryptographically throughout a product's lifecycle. That system became the blueprint for everything that followed, in defense, semiconductors, automotive, and beyond.

A secure product is also a powerful sales differentiator. For a customer investing millions of dollars in a manufacturing process that depends on an industrial control system, a demonstrably secure product represents significantly less risk than a competitor's offering burdened with security advisories. A secure medical device is easier for physicians and hospitals to recommend. A vehicle that cannot be trivially unlocked or stolen is more attractive to consumers, in part because it lowers insurance costs.

The corporate mindset regarding IoT cybersecurity must be reframed.

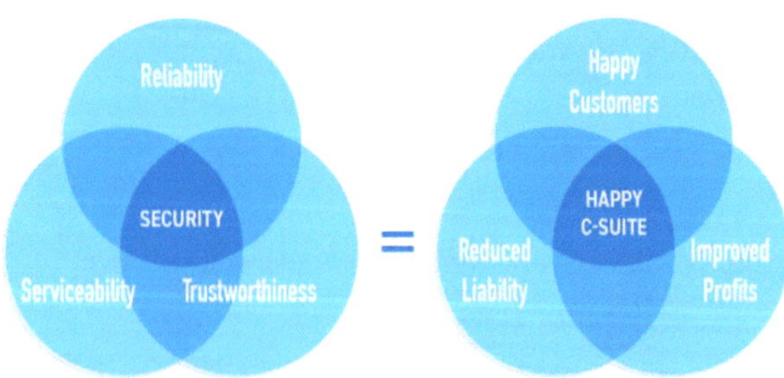

Figure 1: ***The IoT Cybersecurity C-suite Mindset Reframe***

Embedded and IoT Devices

Discussions of cybersecurity typically focus on the policies, procedures, and technical controls used to protect large-scale enterprise IT environments from attack and misuse. While there is significant overlap between enterprise cybersecurity requirements and those for embedded systems, embedded systems have a distinct advantage: because of their focused purpose and constrained design, their attack surfaces are often smaller, and their security controls can be made significantly stronger.

Before proceeding further, it is useful to clarify what we mean by **embedded devices** and **IoT devices**.

Embedded Devices

An embedded device is a self-contained, microprocessor-based system designed to perform dedicated, application-specific functions within a larger product or system. Unlike general-purpose computers, embedded systems typically support a single application—or a very limited set of applications, and are optimized for efficiency, reliability, and tight integration with hardware.

The key characteristics of embedded devices include:

Application-Specific Design

Embedded devices are built to perform one or a small number of dedicated functions, such as vehicle control systems, medical devices, or industrial automation systems. Design priorities are driven by cost, performance, power consumption, and physical size rather than flexibility.

Microprocessor or Microcontroller CPU

The primary, and often only, compute element is a microprocessor or microcontroller selected based on cost and performance requirements. These devices typically integrate the CPU, memory, and peripherals on a single chip, with external memory used only when necessary.

Real-Time Operation

Many embedded systems must respond predictably to external events in near real time. As a result, they often employ real-time operating systems (RTOS) or bare-metal implementations, in which software executes directly on the hardware without a general-purpose operating system.

Resource Constraints

Embedded systems are commonly designed to be low cost and therefore operate under tight constraints on memory, processing capability, and energy consumption.

Reliability and Stability

Designed for continuous operation, embedded devices may run for years without reboot or failure - satellite systems are a classic example. In safety-critical applications such as avionics, automotive systems, and medical equipment, embedded systems are engineered for high reliability and fail-safe operation.

Minimal or No User Interface

Many embedded devices operate with little or no direct user interaction.

Tight Hardware Integration

Embedded systems are closely coupled with sensors, actuators, and other hardware components within the larger system.

Power Efficiency

These devices are often battery-powered or otherwise optimized for low energy consumption.

Embedded Software

Software is typically stored in ROM or flash memory, and updates may be infrequent or, in some cases, impossible. Programs are generally compact and optimized for performance and memory efficiency.

IoT Devices

An IoT (Internet of Things) device is typically an embedded system augmented with sensors, network connectivity, and software that enables it to collect, exchange, and act on data over a network, most often the internet. Examples include smart televisions, electronic control units (ECUs) in vehicles, connected industrial sensors, and drones.

IoT devices share many of the characteristics of embedded devices, but they additionally emphasize the following:

Connectivity

Connectivity is what fundamentally distinguishes an IoT device from a standalone embedded system. IoT devices use networks such as

Ethernet, Wi-Fi, Bluetooth, Zigbee, LoRa, and 5G to exchange data with other devices and backend systems.

Sensing and Data Collection

IoT devices commonly include sensors to measure physical parameters such as temperature, motion, humidity, GPS location, or light. They may also incorporate actuators that allow them to affect the physical world, such as starting motors or opening valves. Data collection may be continuous, periodic, or event-driven.

Autonomy and Remote Operation

IoT devices are designed to operate with minimal human intervention and can be monitored and controlled remotely via applications, dashboards, or APIs. More sophisticated devices, particularly those used in high-value or safety-critical environments, often support secure over-the-air (OTA) firmware updates for maintenance and enhancement.

Interoperability

IoT devices are frequently integrated into larger IoT and IT ecosystems. For example, industrial IoT sensors may connect to an industrial control system (ICS), which in turn interfaces with enterprise IT networks.

Upgradability and Controllability

Because they are network-connected, IoT devices can be remotely configured, managed, and updated throughout their operational lifetimes.

Security

Strong cybersecurity is a critical requirement due to constant network exposure. IoT devices require encryption, authentication, secure boot, and protected firmware update mechanisms. Vulnerabilities in these devices can compromise not only the device itself but also the broader IoT ecosystem and connected enterprise systems.

Application-Specific Functionality

IoT devices are designed for specific domains, such as smart homes, healthcare, agriculture, industrial automation, and logistics, and are tightly integrated into real-world operational processes.

Cybersecurity Challenges: Embedded/IoT vs. Enterprise

While there is overlap in cybersecurity methods and technologies between enterprise IT and embedded or IoT devices, there are also significant differences. These differences arise because embedded devices, with their inherent capability and resource limitations, require and enable unique cybersecurity approaches. An overview contrasting enterprise and embedded cybersecurity is outlined below.

Environment Complexity

Enterprise cybersecurity must protect large-scale, complex IT environments that include servers, endpoints of multiple types, cloud platforms, and corporate networks. It deals with distributed systems, remote users, and business applications. Security efforts focus on managing data flows, user access, identity and authorization, and regulatory compliance.

Embedded system cybersecurity protects special-purpose devices such as industrial controllers, medical devices, automotive electronic control units (ECUs), flight control systems, and defense platforms. These devices are typically deployed in isolated and/or highly resource-constrained environments. Security focuses on ensuring the reliability, integrity, and safety of real-time operations, such as those for autonomous driving, missile guidance, or medical infusion control.

System Constraints

Enterprise IT systems have substantial computing power and storage, making them more tolerant of resource-intensive security controls such as intrusion detection and prevention systems (IDS/IPS), security information and event management (SIEM), endpoint detection and response (EDR), and encryption at rest. Infrastructure, servers, and endpoints generally have relatively short lifecycles, often less than five years, and are regularly upgraded.

Embedded products, by contrast, are both resource-limited and cost-constrained. They typically use low-power CPUs, limited memory, and minimal storage, and they run purpose-built software for a single or small number of applications. As a result, security solutions must be highly optimized for performance and footprint, particularly when real-time operating systems (RTOS) are used and deterministic response times are required. Embedded devices may also have very long lifespans, often 10 to 20 years or more, with limited or no update mechanisms. Certain industrial control platforms, for example, may remain fielded for decades. Additionally, embedded systems are frequently deployed in safety-critical or life-safety applications.

Threats

Threat actors targeting both enterprise and embedded systems are largely similar. Hackers, cybercriminals, and nation-states may seek data theft, ransomware deployment, financial fraud, espionage, or service disruption. Both environments must ensure system availability. However, many embedded and IoT systems must also ensure safe and fail-safe operation, such as preventing the compromise of a vehicle brake ECU.

Attack vectors for both enterprise and embedded systems include firmware and software tampering, supply chain attacks, remote exploitation, and physical attacks. A key difference is that enterprise IT assets are typically located in controlled environments where physical and procedural protections can be applied. IoT devices, by contrast, are often deployed in the field, exposed to physical access and environmental risks. The large number and geographically distributed nature of IoT devices further complicates protection, monitoring, and recovery following an attack.

Update and Lifecycle Management

Enterprise IT environments benefit from regular, centralized, and automated patching and software updates. Endpoint management tools are commonly used to enforce security policies and compliance across the organization.

Embedded systems, particularly those deployed in isolated environments with limited or no connectivity, rely heavily on secure boot mechanisms and code signing to maintain system integrity and trustworthy operation. Historically, firmware updates were rare or infeasible once devices were deployed. In modern systems, over-the-air (OTA) updates are becoming more common, but customized and carefully controlled update mechanisms are still required, especially for devices that are intermittently connected or completely offline.

Security Mechanisms

Enterprise security measures are diverse, compute-intensive, and often dependent on third-party tools and services. These include firewalls, SIEM platforms, intrusion detection and prevention systems, endpoint protection, zero trust architectures, data loss prevention, and multifactor authentication (MFA). Enterprise cybersecurity strategies often emphasize protecting sensitive data and critical servers by surrounding them with layered external defenses.

Embedded security, due to CPU, memory, and cost constraints, focuses primarily on securing the endpoint device itself and its associated command-and-control systems, if present. This includes hardware-based security capabilities such as secure boot, hardware security modules (HSMs), unique device identities, encryption, authentication, and tamper resistance. For safety-critical applications, a secure or safety-certified operating system may be used to ensure reliable and predictable operation.

Summary

In summary, enterprise cybersecurity is centered on protecting data-rich, compute-intensive, and dynamic IT environments from a broad range of digital threats. Cybersecurity for embedded systems, including those that comprise the Internet of Things, focuses on protecting resource-constrained devices that often run real-time and/or safety-critical applications, while also safeguarding sensitive data from compromise or manipulation. Examples include autonomous vehicles, industrial control systems, and home video surveillance devices.

The Ever-Expanding Attack Surface

Fear and Loathing in the C-Suite

Just as the physical universe is known to be expanding, the attack surface of IoT products and their associated services is expanding as well. Unlike the universe, whose growth is driven by dark energy, the expansion of the IoT attack surface is driven by the increasing complexity of devices themselves and by the additional infrastructure required to manufacture, deploy, and operate them. Corporate and engineering leadership must recognize and adapt to this changing environment or risk being caught unprepared.

Hackers often view products the way children view a chocolate-covered nougat candy: crunchy on the outside with a soft, rewarding center. In the enterprise, perimeter defenses form the crunchy exterior, while valuable data sits at the center as the prize. Embedded devices, however, typically have well-defined interfaces and narrowly scoped applications. This allows security controls to be tightly integrated into the product itself, creating a much thicker and stronger protective layer. As a result, the cybersecurity posture of well-designed embedded products can, in many cases, be significantly stronger than what is achievable in enterprise IT environments.

Why Do Good Products Go Bad?

Having spent more than 60 combined years in this field, it is clear to us that good products do not fail on their own; they usually fail with help. *First and foremost, cybersecurity is treated as an afterthought rather than as a standard design requirement from the outset.* It remains distressing how many products and services with weak security controls continue to be brought to market. Default or fixed passwords are still hard-coded into software. Flawed protocol implementations are shipped. Backward compatibility is prioritized over the security vulnerabilities it introduces. There is often little understanding of how cryptographic choices relate to data sensitivity and product lifetimes. Worse still, many systems continue to rely on non-vetted proprietary techniques under the false assumption of "security through obscurity."

A concrete example illustrates this point. In August 2025, the U.S. Cybersecurity and Infrastructure Security Agency (CISA) released nine industrial control systems (ICS) security advisories. The reported vulnerabilities included buffer overflows, improper FTP input validation, lack of cryptographic protection for remote control, flawed password generation based on date and time, improper handling of special elements, incorrect length handling in embedded web servers, insufficient command privilege control, and uncontrolled search paths. In at least one case, a vendor advised customers that no fixed version would be released, leaving equipment replacement as the only option to improve cybersecurity posture. The takeaway is clear: these vulnerabilities did not need to exist had cybersecurity been properly addressed throughout the product lifecycle. Poor cybersecurity hygiene rarely strengthens customer relations.

At the same time, increasing CPU performance, dramatic growth in chip functionality, and ubiquitous device connectivity across a widening range of protocols (for example, Wi-Fi, cellular, automotive, aviation, industrial and electrical buses, NFC, TCP/IP (IPv4/IPv6), and Bluetooth) have significantly increased both hardware and software complexity. Software complexity is not driven solely by added functionality, but also by how software is developed. Open-source code authored by unknown contributors is now embedded in many products. Many consumers are unaware that their television or home router likely runs on Linux. Are your development teams fully confident they understand the functionality and security implications of that code?

Development and operational environments have increasingly moved to the cloud. Organizations must ask whether unauthorized individuals have access to these environments and whether the code within them can be trusted. Artificial intelligence is now generating product software, raising further questions about whether its output adheres to secure development best practices. The net result is an ever-expanding IoT attack surface that is becoming increasingly difficult to secure.

The *ENISA Threat Landscape 2025* report provides a comprehensive overview of this growing attack surface. Although not focused exclusively on embedded systems, many of its findings are directly applicable to IoT products and their supporting operational environments. The report analyzed 4,875 incidents occurring between 1 July 2024 and 30 June 2025. During this period, 42,595 new vulnerabilities were disclosed, of which 7% were rated Critical and 26% High.

The report notes that social engineering remains the primary entry point for attackers, with phishing techniques, including vishing, malspam, and malvertising, accounting for approximately 60% of observed cases. Exploitation of vulnerabilities followed at 21.3%, with botnets representing 9.9%. Botnets are frequently built by compromising consumer IoT devices such as home routers. Malicious applications accounted for 8% of incidents, demonstrating the continued role of trojanized or compromised software. Insider threats contributed a smaller but still relevant share at 0.8%. Overall, nearly 70% of vulnerability cases led to successful intrusions, with data breaches (68.6%) and data exfiltration (30.2%) being the most common outcomes.

Figure 2 illustrates the distribution of threats as identified in the report. In this context, Operational Technology (OT) refers to industrial and other critical systems that are often interconnected with enterprise networks and increasingly targeted by adversaries. These OT environments are built on embedded IoT devices, reinforcing the importance of addressing cybersecurity at the device level.

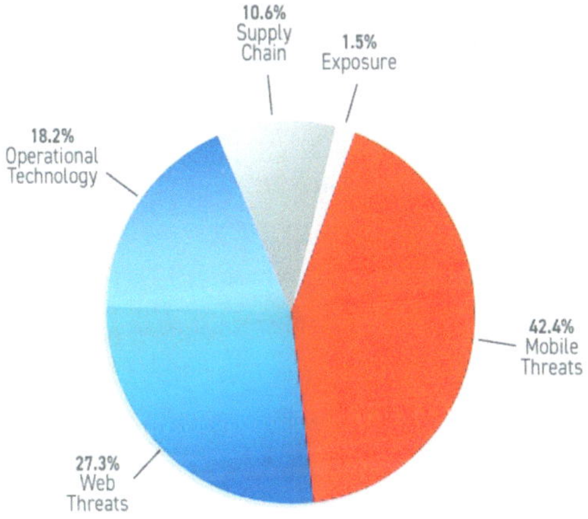

Figure 2: ***Distribution of Threats (see ENISA Threat Landscape)***

While there had been earlier attacks on operational technology environments, the Stuxnet malware was the first to demonstrate to a global audience the extent of physical damage that a cyberattack could inflict on industrial systems. Discovered in the late 2000s, Stuxnet is widely attributed to the United States and Israel, who sought to prevent Iran from enriching uranium for a potential nuclear weapons program.

Stuxnet was specifically crafted to target certain Siemens supervisory control and data acquisition (SCADA) systems and programmable logic controllers (PLCs), along with the associated STEP 7 programming and configuration software. These systems were used to control the uranium enrichment centrifuges at Iran's nuclear facilities. Although Iran had isolated its OT networks from external connectivity, attackers nonetheless found a pathway to introduce the malware into the Siemens-controlled environment.

Once deployed, Stuxnet caused the Siemens PLCs to manipulate centrifuge rotational speeds in irregular and difficult-to-diagnose patterns. Specifically, the malware altered the frequency converters driving the centrifuges from their normal operating frequency of 1,064 Hz to 1,410 Hz for 15 minutes, then returned them to 1,064 Hz for 26 days. After this period, it reduced the frequency to 2 Hz for 50 minutes before resetting it again to normal operation for another 26 days, after which the cycle repeated. Critically, Stuxnet also modified monitoring systems to falsely report normal operating conditions to plant operators. The repeated stress from these speed fluctuations resulted in the physical destruction of centrifuges. Evidence suggests that Stuxnet may also have interfered with valves controlling the flow of uranium hexafluoride gas within and between centrifuge cascades, further contributing to equipment damage.

The financial implications of such attacks are profound. According to Dragos' *2025 OT Security Financial Risk Report*, OT cyber incidents are expected to generate more than $31.1 billion in global financial risk in 2026 alone, excluding any filed business interruption (BI) claims. In extreme tail-risk scenarios, that figure rises to an estimated $329 billion globally. Indirect costs, including precautionary shutdowns, cascading supply chain impacts, and prolonged recovery efforts, account for approximately 70% of total OT breach costs and often exceed direct losses.

Returning to the ENISA Threat Landscape report, Figure 2 highlights supply chain attacks as a major threat vector. In these attacks, adversaries exploit indirect pathways through third-party vendors, service providers, and software dependencies to compromise target systems. As a result, an organization's attack surface now extends well beyond its own boundaries into its ecosystem of suppliers and partners, including open-source communities. It is highly likely that your organization relies on such third parties in both operations and product development. When customers deploy your products, they may inherit exposure to these same attack vectors.

An early and well-known example of a supply chain compromise occurred in 2013 with the breach of Target's point-of-sale (POS) systems. Attackers first compromised a third-party HVAC contractor and stole network credentials. Using those credentials, they accessed Target's internal network and deployed malware on POS terminals, resulting in the theft of millions of payment card records.

The supply chain attack that truly spurred global awareness was the 2020 SolarWinds compromise. SolarWinds' Orion platform, used by more than 30,000 organizations, provided automated IT infrastructure monitoring and management, including configuration changes, updates, and policy enforcement across on-premises and cloud environments. Nation-state attackers gained access to SolarWinds' internal build environment and inserted a backdoor into a legitimate Orion dynamic link library (DLL), which was then digitally signed and distributed as part of a trusted software update. Because the malicious DLL was properly signed, customer systems accepted it as authentic. Once deployed, the backdoor enabled attackers to deliver additional malware, forge privileged credentials, move laterally within victim networks, and exfiltrate sensitive data. This attack is attributed to Cozy Bear, an advanced persistent threat (APT) group linked to Russian foreign intelligence. Ultimately, more than 18,000 organizations were compromised, including the U.S. Treasury, the Department of Homeland Security, and the National Security Agency. The scale of the attack was unprecedented, eliminating any notion of a one-to-one relationship between attacker and target.

Another deeply concerning category of supply chain attack leverages open-source software, which is now embedded in most modern products. Using stolen credentials, attackers gain access to repositories such as GitHub and inject malicious code into widely used libraries. A striking example was documented by Akido Security BV on September 8, 2025, when they identified unauthorized packages uploaded to npm, the package manager for Node.js. These packages contained malicious code capable of silently intercepting cryptocurrency and Web3 activity within users' browsers, manipulating wallet interactions, and redirecting payments to attacker-controlled accounts without obvious user-visible indicators. Alarmingly, the affected packages collectively recorded more than two billion downloads per week. This incident highlights not only the risks inherent in open-source supply chains, but also the dangers introduced by modern continuous integration and continuous deployment (CI/CD) pipelines, which can automatically pull compromised dependencies into production code. As a result, repositories such as npm represent extremely high-value targets for attackers, enabling malware propagation across thousands of projects and potentially millions of devices. Nation-state actors, including North Korea, are known to be active in this space.

The ENISA report also emphasizes the growing threat of ransomware, noting that cybercriminals primarily target manufacturing organizations and digital infrastructure and service providers. In the United States, healthcare systems and critical infrastructure such as telecommunications providers and municipal utilities have been frequent victims.

The automotive industry, in particular, has become a significant ransomware target. According to RSM International Ltd., "ransomware-related costs in the automotive sector increased from $74.7 million to $209.6 million in the first half of 2023" alone, while system downtime reached an estimated $1.99 billion for the year. These figures are overshadowed by the August 2025 ransomware attack by the Scattered Lapsus$ Hunters group against Jaguar Land Rover (JLR). The attack halted JLR's global production, disrupted approximately 5,000 downstream businesses, and sent shockwaves through the supplier ecosystem, pushing many companies to the brink of insolvency. The UK government ultimately underwrote a loan guarantee exceeding £1.5 billion to help JLR support its suppliers. The total economic impact of the attack is estimated at approximately £1.9 billion.

AI Is Not Your Friend

Artificial intelligence (AI) is increasingly being leveraged by attackers to create new attack techniques and to refine existing ones, such as phishing. Most critically, AI enables attacks to be scaled cost-effectively. According to the ENISA report, more than 80% of phishing emails now leverage AI-generated content. Deep-fake websites, voice-based phishing (vishing), and fake GitHub repositories are all increasingly powered by AI. AI is also being used to develop malware designed to evade reconnaissance, detection, and anomaly-based defenses.

One example is *BlackMamba*, which leverages ChatGPT to generate a polymorphic keylogger dynamically at runtime. Each execution produces a modified version of the malware, allowing it to evade traditional antivirus and endpoint protection systems that rely on signature-based detection.

Anthropic has documented a wide range of nation-state and cybercriminal misuse of its Claude AI model. Their findings show that threat actors are increasingly incorporating AI across the full lifecycle of cyber operations, from planning and reconnaissance to execution and monetization. In its August 2025 *Threat Intelligence Report*, Anthropic identified the following patterns of malicious AI usage:

- **Weaponization of agentic AI systems.** AI models are being used directly to carry out sophisticated cyberattacks, rather than merely advising human operators.
- **Lower barriers to advanced cybercrime.** Individuals with limited technical expertise are using AI to conduct complex attacks, such as ransomware development, that previously required years of training.
- **End-to-end integration of AI in cyber operations.** Threat actors embed AI into victim profiling, automated service delivery, and campaigns affecting tens of thousands of users.
- **AI-driven fraud at scale.** AI is used throughout fraud operations, including analyzing stolen data, harvesting credit card information, and generating synthetic identities.

Claude has been used to develop ransomware and to enable ransomware-as-a-service offerings. This included automating target reconnaissance and discovery, providing real-time operational assistance during attacks, facilitating data exfiltration of sensitive information (including account data, patient records, and export-controlled documentation), and generating extortion demands and phishing emails. AI allowed attackers to extract high-value data simultaneously across multiple victim organizations.

In September 2025, Anthropic detected a well-funded, Chinese state-sponsored group using Claude to target approximately 30 organizations, successfully compromising a subset of them. This campaign was notable for its *"unprecedented integration and autonomy of AI throughout the attack lifecycle."* Claude was reportedly used across nearly every phase of the operation, from reconnaissance and vulnerability discovery to exploitation, lateral movement, data analysis, and exfiltration. Anthropic described this as *"the first documented case of agentic AI successfully obtaining access to confirmed high-value targets for intelligence collection, including major technology companies and government agencies."*

Additional documented uses of Claude during 2025 include:

- **North Korea** using AI to place operatives as IT workers inside target companies, as well as creating malware distribution campaigns via phishing lures on LinkedIn and GitHub. Claude was also used to generate malicious npm packages.
- **China** leveraging Claude to enhance cyber operations targeting Vietnamese critical infrastructure.
- **Cybercriminal groups** using Claude to build malware with advanced evasion techniques, analyze credential-stealer logs, construct detailed victim profiles, and enhance financial card fraud services.

In a further escalation, at least one hacker has developed a bespoke AI platform, *Xanthorox AI*, built from the ground up for offensive cyber operations (despite their disclaimers to the contrary). Meanwhile, CISA and the NSA have warned that organizations training AI models on control-process data, such as voltage, temperature, pressure, and mass-flow rates, risk unintended data retention that could expose intellectual property and sensitive operational patterns.

These machine-speed, virtually autonomous attacks represent a significant amplification of the IoT attack surface, given AI's ability to rapidly discover vulnerabilities and exploit them at scale. It is also important to recognize that while many organizations are using AI to assist in software development, current AI systems are not known to produce consistently secure code. As a result, the overall attack surface is not being reduced. Moreover, AI platforms integrated into enterprise environments introduce new attack surfaces, as AI software itself is not immune to vulnerabilities.

Perhaps Stanley Kubrick foreshadowed this dynamic in *2001: A Space Odyssey*, when HAL, the AI computer, calmly declared, *"I'm sorry, Dave, I'm afraid I can't do that,"* as it locked a human out of a spacecraft drifting through space.

The Embedded/IoT Cybersecurity Strategy

How can you successfully address an ever-changing product attack surface and mitigate the potential impact of a successful attack against your company and its customers? Based on the authors' experience delivering innovative, cost-effective security solutions across multiple industries, this book presents a best-practices approach for developing a practical and actionable embedded/IoT cybersecurity strategy.

At a high level, this strategy comprises four conceptual steps:

1. **Understand the full product lifecycle**

   Thoroughly identify how your product will be specified, manufactured, deployed, operated, maintained, and ultimately decommissioned. A secure product strategy begins with a complete understanding of its lifecycle.

2. **Identify and classify critical assets**

   Determine which product assets, such as sensitive data, cryptographic keys, user accounts, firmware, and cloud services, require protection from both inadvertent misuse and deliberate attack.

3. **Define the security architecture**

   Create a security architecture specification that governs the design and implementation of your embedded/IoT products and their supporting services across the entire lifecycle.

4. **Ensure secure implementation and operation**

Verify that the product and its associated services are implemented correctly and operated securely so they remain dependable, resilient, and trustworthy throughout their operational lifetimes.

Although written from a high-level perspective, this book provides sufficient depth for C-suite leaders and senior executives to understand:

- The steps required to define a practical product cybersecurity strategy;
- The security capabilities that must be built into embedded/IoT products;
- The rationale behind key design decisions;
- The supporting services required to maintain security over the product's lifetime; and
- How to guide their organizations toward a lifecycle-based view of product security.

What do we mean by the product lifecycle? The lifecycle encompasses every phase of a product's existence, from initial concept and specification, through design and manufacturing, to deployment, operation, maintenance, and ultimately end-of-life decommissioning (Figure 3).

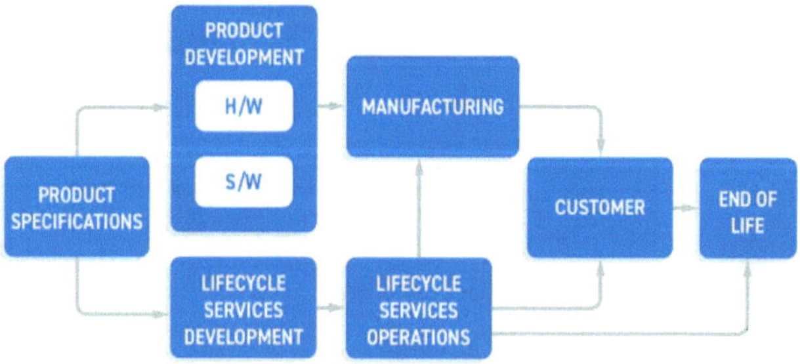

Figure 3: **The Product Lifecycle**

Each of the blocks in Figure 3 has its own distinct security concerns that must be addressed. For example, during development, portions of the work may be outsourced to third parties. Does your team have visibility into their development environments, the open-source software they use to build your product or supporting services, and their IT security practices? If your developers are using AI-assisted coding tools, how do you verify that the resulting code meets acceptable security standards?

Manufacturing may also be partially or fully outsourced. How will your intellectual property, such as gold firmware images, be protected in third-party environments? How will highly sensitive data, including cryptographic keys, be handled on an external manufacturing line, protected from compromise, and injected only into authorized products? Are the manufacturer's test systems connected to networks that also interface with enterprise IT systems or the internet? How do you ensure that a contract manufacturer is not producing unauthorized overruns or cloning your products? How can your custom chip's JTAG interface be securely unlocked only at authorized service locations, while keeping on-chip secrets protected?

Once deployed at customer sites, additional concerns arise. How can you be confident that your product can reliably generate strong cryptographic keys? How do you ensure that your over-the-air (OTA) update system distributes only authorized, authentic firmware, and only to legitimate devices? How do you guarantee that a failed OTA update does not leave a device inoperable or unsafe?

At end-of-life (EOL), the risks continue. For many consumer products, EOL simply involves disposal. However, higher-value products containing sensitive data, such as persistent storage in laptops, industrial control system (ICS) logic and data, or autonomous driving firmware, may require secure data erasure and electronic disablement to prevent reuse, reverse engineering, or misuse.

A properly implemented cybersecurity strategy for embedded products protects your company's reputation, safeguards your customers, and mitigates legal and financial liability. Beyond risk reduction, strong product cybersecurity can also enable new revenue streams by supporting secure content licensing, feature activation and monetization, controlled product servicing, and protection against unauthorized or counterfeit accessories and replacement parts.

Failing to treat cybersecurity as a fundamental product requirement, rather than an afterthought, can lead to severe unintended consequences following a compromise. Worse, once embedded products are in production and deployed, adding adequate cybersecurity controls is often prohibitively expensive or technically infeasible.

History provides ample examples of such failures. During the conflict with al-Qaeda in Afghanistan, the United States deployed surveillance drones whose live video feeds were intercepted using freely available software, as reported by *Al Jazeera* on December 19, 2009. The interception was possible because the communications links to the remotely piloted aircraft were unencrypted. Remediating the issue required updating approximately 600 drones and thousands of ground stations.

Similarly, the previously discussed 2015 Jeep Cherokee attack by Charlie Miller and Chris Valasek resulted in a recall of 1.4 million Fiat Chrysler vehicles, costing the company millions of dollars.

More recently, in September 2025, *The Register* reported that a software-defined radio could remotely trigger emergency braking and derail a U.S. train. Although the vulnerability was first identified in 2012, advances in technology have made it far easier to exploit. According to the Association of American Railroads, *"there is no solution to this vulnerability,"* and mitigation will require adoption of *"newer, more secure technology."*

Hopefully, this has made clear the importance of addressing cybersecurity across the entire product lifecycle. With that foundation established, we can now begin the process.

Commencing the Security Architecture Specification

A commercial or residential architect must first specify a building's requirements (for example, five stories, 80 offices) before creating detailed construction blueprints. This process also includes ensuring compliance with the applicable building codes for the location in which the structure will be built. These codes vary between residential and commercial buildings and differ by county and country.

This process is analogous to the development of a product's cybersecurity architecture. Only after defining what must be protected, along with the relevant threats and vulnerabilities, can an effective cybersecurity architecture be specified. A complete Security Architecture Specification (SAS) encompasses not only the product itself, but also its manufacturing environment, operational environment, and end-of-life decommissioning. Required protection standards may differ across commercial, consumer, and defense markets, as well as by the countries in which the product or service will be sold and used.

Your A-Team

The first step is to assemble your SAS team to review the intended product and lead the development of the Security Architecture Specification. This team must be multidisciplinary and include representatives from any group within the company that may be impacted by, or involved with, the product. These stakeholders ensure that security considerations are integrated across the organization. At this stage, the product management team typically represents the customer, unless the product is being developed

Commencing the Security Architecture Specification collaboratively with external partners. Based on our experience, the SAS team should include members from human resources, software and hardware engineering, IT and OT, manufacturing, repair services, customer support, finance, legal, and executive management. The product, its data, and its usage will likely touch all of these groups.

The team should be led by an embedded cybersecurity expert with a deep understanding of secure embedded devices, their operating environments, their manufacturing processes, and their supporting infrastructure, such as over-the-air update systems.

Once the SAS stakeholder team is identified, the following documentation should be gathered:

- Marketing and engineering product specifications,
- Applicable government and third-party standards and regulations,
- Product use cases,
- High-level functional design documentation,
- Initial component selections, and
- Cost-of-goods target.

Using this information, the team can develop the Security Architecture Specification by following the steps outlined below and illustrated in Figure 4:

- Specify and verify the use cases the product or service must support, along with any known security attributes (for example, an airborne system must transmit confidential video to ground stations). These use cases should include functional details so that data flows and storage locations can be identified.

- Identify the critical assets used by the product or service and define their required security attributes (for example, a video stream must remain confidential, be protected against alteration or substitution, and allow the receiver to verify the authenticity of the source).
- Identify potential threat actors, along with their skill levels and available resources.
- Identify product and service vulnerabilities affecting critical assets and the threats that could exploit them.
- Assess the risk to both the company and its customers if those vulnerabilities are successfully exploited.
- Specify the security controls required to mitigate the vulnerabilities and reduce risk to an acceptable level.
- Define the cybersecurity architecture concept requirements necessary to implement the identified security controls.
- Ensure that the secure product meets the cost-of-goods-sold (COGS) target.

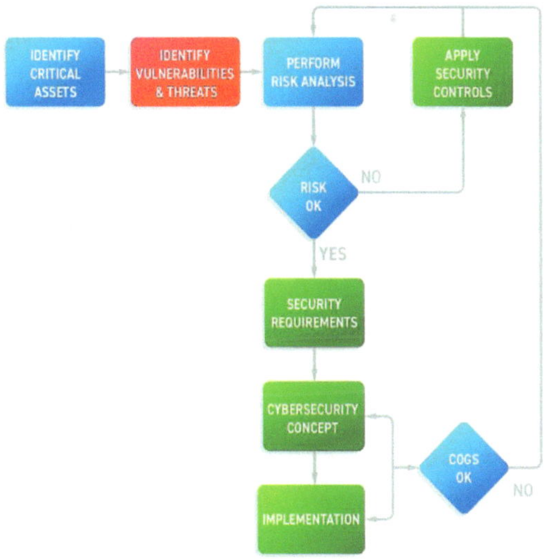

Figure 4: ***The Security Architecture Specification Process***

This is an iterative process as multiple security controls may be required to fully eliminate threats or reduce them to an acceptable level of risk. A similar approach can be applied to safety-critical devices, where fail-safe operation and fault tolerance must be analyzed and appropriate safety controls implemented.

This security architecture specification process should be followed in as much detail as possible to identify and eliminate security flaws across a product's design, development, manufacturing, and operational phases.

Determining Your Critical Assets and Their Lifetimes

This step identifies the assets that underpin your IoT device and its supporting systems, as well as which of those assets require protection. These protected assets are referred to as *critical assets*. In the physical world, we are all familiar with assets that must be protected against compromise or theft, such as bank accounts, credit cards, jewelry, or a prized classic automobile. The same concept applies in the digital domain. Assets that are critical to corporate revenue and liability and those associated with product's design, manufacture, reliable operation, and application data handling must be identified so they can be protected appropriately.

Examples of these primarily digital assets include, but are not limited to, the following:

- Intellectual property;
- Firmware and software (bootloader, operating system, application software), including the software development environment and packages (DevSecOps environment), as well as future updates and patches;
- Cryptographic material (keys, random number generator state);
- Commands and messages exchanged between product subsystems;
- Commands and messages exchanged between the product and its ecosystem (for example, IoT servers and third-party systems), including command and control, feature enablement, and software updates;
- Identity and authorization data (operator credentials, OAuth tokens, device certificates);
- Data, including product feature data, control values (for example, calibration data, valve positions, process temperatures), personally identifiable information (PII), customer data, and financial information;
- Open-source software and repositories;
- Contract manufacturer test programs;
- Product and service availability;
- Module, subassembly, and component provenance;
- Open-source and licensed software;

- Product and service revenue streams; and
- Intangible assets such as reputation, customer loyalty, goodwill, and brand equity.

The asset identification process requires a multidisciplinary team, as the product development team may not be fully aware of the composition or operation of supporting elements such as enterprise or cloud IT systems, or third-party contract manufacturing and test environments. The final list of critical assets should exclude assets that are not fundamental to the secure and reliable operation of the product, as those assets do not require explicit protection.

Once the critical assets have been identified, their useful lifetimes must be determined so that appropriate protection mechanisms can be applied. For example, healthcare data may require protection for a duration comparable to an individual's lifetime. A financial transaction, such as a stock purchase, may only require protection for a few seconds. A digital key used to unlock and start a vehicle may need to remain secure for more than a decade.

Asset lifetimes directly influence the selection and implementation of protection methods. For instance, a large quantity of gold bullion requires physical protection comparable to that of Fort Knox, whereas wire transfer instructions require protection of the data itself, along with assurance that the instructions cannot be replayed, counterfeited, or altered.

Understanding the Threat Agent Universe

Having identified your critical assets and their associated lifetimes, the next step is to consider the threat agents who may act against you or your customers. A threat against an asset typically requires a malicious actor to carry it out, unless it results from a natural disaster or an "act of God."

In this section, the universe of potential threat agents is examined, including their technical sophistication, financial resources, and motivations for conducting an attack. The table describing the Threat Agent Universe (Table 1) is derived from a paper presented at the 2017 ESCAR Conference in Berlin (Karahasanovic & Kelberger, 2017).

Not all of these threat agents or attack types will be applicable to every product or service. However, taken together, they represent a comprehensive view of the malicious attack landscape that organizations should consider when developing a robust cybersecurity strategy.

Threat Agent Attributes		Non-Hostile Intent			Hostile Intent											
		Reckless Employee	Untrained Employee	Commercial Partner	Competitor	Data Miner	Script Kiddies	Nation-state Hacker	Organized Crime	Hacktivist	Hacker	Cyber Terrorist	Cybercriminal	Nation-state Spy	Internal Spy	Disgruntled Employee
Access	Internal	✓	✓	✓										✓	✓	✓
	External				✓	✓	✓	✓	✓	✓	✓	✓	✓	✓		
Outcome	Acquisition/Theft				✓		✓		✓		✓		✓	✓	✓	✓
	Business Advantage				✓	✓								✓		
	Material Damage	✓	✓					✓	✓	✓		✓	✓			
	Reputation Damage	✓	✓	✓			✓	✓	✓	✓	✓	✓	✓			✓
	Technical Advantage				✓									✓	✓	
	15 Minutes of Fame						✓				✓					
Resources	Individual	✓	✓	✓			✓				✓					✓
	Team					✓					✓					
	Organization				✓				✓	✓		✓	✓		✓	
	Government							✓						✓		
Skills	Minimal		✓				✓									
	Operational	✓		✓							✓		✓			✓
	Adept				✓	✓		✓	✓	✓		✓		✓	✓	
Visibility	Overt	✓	✓	✓					✓	✓	✓		✓			
	Covert	✓							✓	✓	✓	✓	✓		✓	
	Clandestine				✓	✓		✓						✓		
	Don't Care						✓	✓								✓
Limits	Limited Financial	✓	✓	✓			✓				✓					✓
	Moderate Financial				✓	✓			✓	✓		✓	✓		✓	
	Unlimited Financial							✓						✓		
Objective	Copy				✓	✓			✓	✓	✓			✓	✓	
	Deny						✓	✓			✓	✓				
	Injure							✓				✓		✓		
	Destroy							✓	✓	✓		✓				✓
	Damage							✓	✓	✓	✓	✓		✓		✓
	Take							✓				✓		✓		
	All the Above/Don't Care	✓	✓	✓			✓						✓			
Motivation	Accidental	✓	✓	✓												
	Coercion								✓				✓			
	Dominance							✓								
	Ideology									✓		✓		✓		
	Notoriety						✓				✓					
	Operational Gain				✓	✓		✓	✓					✓		
	Disgruntlement															✓
	Financial Gain					✓		✓	✓				✓	✓	✓	
	Personal Satisfaction						✓									

Table 1: **Threat Agent Universe**

This table categorizes threats using the following attributes:

- **Intent** describes whether the threat agent intends to cause harm or not.

- **Access** describes the starting point for the threat agent's attack. Many attackers begin outside the organization and subsequently move internally within an organization or laterally across organizations.
- **Outcome** indicates the final results of the attack. A single attack may result in multiple outcomes.
- **Resources** indicate the sophistication of the attack. Collaboration with others increases the likelihood of success, and larger group sizes are often indicative of greater financial backing.
- **Skills** describe the technical skill set of the threat agent.
- **Visibility** characterizes how detectable the attack is. Some attacks provide immediate evidence of compromise, while others, particularly those conducted by nation-states, may remain hidden for long periods.
- **Limits** describe the financial constraints (or lack thereof) of the threat agent.
- **Objective** defines the threat agent's goals in conducting the attack.
- **Motivation** describes the rationale driving the attack and is also an indicator of the time, technical, and financial resources likely to be applied.

Let us now discuss several representative threat agents, beginning with nation-state actors with hostile intent, listed in approximate order of decreasing resources.

- **Nation-State Hacker / Spy**: Nation-state threat actors possess deep technical expertise and potentially very large budgets. They may also operate with extremely long and patient timelines. These actors are commonly referred to as *Advanced Persistent Threats (APTs)*. Their objectives may include stealing intellectual property, corrupting the operation of products or services, or planting backdoors for future disruption of critical services. Historical examples include the Soviet space shuttle program, which used stolen NASA designs, and the rapid development of Chinese stealth fighters following the theft of sensitive design information from U.S. defense contractors. North Korea is also known to fund state activities in part through large-scale cryptocurrency theft.

- **Data Miner**: Data miners leverage observable data, often from indirect or nontraditional sources, to inform financial or strategic decisions. Examples include estimating oil reserves by observing storage tank levels from aerial imagery, analyzing crop yields using satellite data, or inferring mergers and acquisitions by examining communication patterns between senior executives. Given the large sums of money involved, these actors often have access to significant technical and financial resources.

- **Competitor / Internal Spy**: Competitors may attempt to steal intellectual property to shorten development cycles or to produce counterfeit parts for gray-market distribution. Hardware designs can be reverse engineered from genuine products, while up-to-date software, calibration files, or configuration data may be accessed via OTA systems or extracted from legitimately acquired devices. A well-known historical example is Cisco's lawsuit against Huawei for the theft and use of Cisco's IOS software in Huawei's products. More recently, North Korea has been documented placing its agents inside companies of interest as IT staff.

- **Organized Crime / Cybercriminal**: Organized crime groups and cybercriminals now represent one of the most active threat categories, driven largely by the widespread use of ransomware. Pre-packaged, ready-to-execute attacks are readily available on the dark web, enabling rapid deployment.

These groups generate millions of dollars in revenue and create severe operational challenges for IT teams and C-suites alike. Easy to penetrate IoT devices are frequently exploited for botnet-based denial-of-service (DoS) attacks, intellectual property theft, and operational disruption. There is increasing overlap and collaboration between these groups and nation-state actors.

- **Hacker**: In this context, hackers are individuals or small groups with limited funding whose goals may include stealing information or damaging operations and reputations. This category overlaps with Script Kiddies, who rely primarily on pre-packaged tools, and Cybercriminals, some of whom are well organized, highly skilled, and well-funded.

- **Cyber Terrorist**: Cyber terrorists are ideologically motivated actors intent on causing business disruption, social instability, or widespread fear by targeting critical services. Some of these groups may be sponsored or supported by nation-states seeking to destabilize adversaries indirectly.

- **Hacktivist**: Hacktivists conduct attacks to make political or social statements or to spread disruption and misinformation. A recent example includes pro-Russian hacktivist groups spreading disinformation related to the Russia–Ukraine war.

In addition to hostile actors, organizations must also guard against unintentional harm caused by **Reckless Employees, Untrained Employees, and Commercial Partners**. These actors may inadvertently disclose sensitive information, misuse systems, or fall victim to social-engineering and phishing attacks. Phishing is particularly dangerous, as it often provides attackers with legitimate credentials that enable deeper compromise.

Commencing the Security Architecture Specification

The BBC reported in September 2025 on an incident in which an organized cybercriminal group attempted to recruit a BBC reporter, offering him a share of the ransom proceeds in exchange for installing malware and disclosing login credentials. Although the reporter refused, the case highlights the strong financial incentives used by criminal organizations ("You'll never have to work again").

Today, ransomware-driven cybercriminal activity is widespread, as evidenced by frequent public reports of attacks against hospitals, airports, automotive manufacturers, and other organizations. Due to the large ransoms frequently paid by their victims, these attackers are highly motivated, well-funded, and increasingly skilled. Artificial intelligence is further amplifying their capabilities by enabling the creation of highly convincing phishing emails, identifying system weaknesses, and even generating exploit code. As a result, traditional cues such as poor grammar or spelling can no longer be relied upon to identify malicious emails.

Threats posed by nation-states are also frequently underestimated at the C-suite level. Embedded and IoT products used in critical infrastructure, such as industrial control systems, telecommunications, transportation, and internet backbone infrastructure, are of particular interest to malicious nation-state actors. Similarly, products capable of disrupting daily life, including autonomous vehicles, traffic signaling systems, and HVAC infrastructure, are attractive targets. While nation-states were once thought to focus primarily on military and defense systems, this assumption is no longer valid. Cyberattacks targeting civilian infrastructure and the general public have been repeatedly documented, such as those against the mobile phone networks and water utilities by APTs. Given the potentially unlimited resources of nation-state attackers, cybersecurity protections must be carefully designed, thoroughly specified, and rigorously implemented.

To capture the diversity of the threat universe while maintaining a manageable framework for conducting a Threat and Risk Assessment, we distill the threat agent categories into those shown in Table 2.

Attacker	Time Resources	Financial Resources
Hacker	Unlimited	Limited
Insider	Limited (months)	Limited
Organized Crime	Limited (months)	<$500K
Industrial Espionage	Many (<10 Person Years)	<$1M
Nation-State	Significant (100s Person Years)	Significant (>$1M)

Table 2: **Summarized Threat Universe**

Artificial Intelligence will increase the capabilities of all threat actors by enabling attackers to deploy existing exploits more efficiently and to uncover zero-day vulnerabilities, both at a fraction of the cost of traditional attacks.

Performing the Threat and Risk Analysis (TARA)

The next step in the security architecture process is to perform a Threat and Risk Analysis (TARA) using the identified critical assets and their associated functional use cases. The TARA process identifies potential vulnerabilities and associated threats to the critical assets that comprise an IoT product and its supporting systems. It then assesses the risk, defined as the potential damage to the business or customer, should those threats be successfully exploited.

In essence, a TARA defines the *attack surface* of an IoT device and its associated systems and provides insight into the consequences of exploitation.

Before examining the TARA process in detail, it is useful to define several key terms:

- **Stakeholder**: A stakeholder is an entity that can affect or be affected by the reliable and trustworthy operation of the product. Examples include your company (from both reputational and financial liability perspectives) and your customer. Within your organization, additional stakeholders may include engineering, marketing, legal, finance, manufacturing, and customer or warranty support. Depending on how your product is deployed, your customer may also have downstream stakeholders, such as their own customers who rely on a product incorporating your device.

- **Threat**: A threat is the potential occurrence of an event that can have an undesirable impact on an asset. Threats may be intentionally malicious, such as an attack on product calibration data, or unintentional, such as water damage to a data center or radiation exposure in a spacecraft. Threats to product assets are analogous to environmental threats a building must be designed to withstand such as hurricanes, earthquakes, or forced entry. A threat is always directed at one or more assets so threats and assets are inherently linked. Not all threats are consequential; the objective is to identify those that are both credible and high-impact.

- **Vulnerability**: A vulnerability is any weakness or deficiency in the product or service, including its design environment, manufacturing process, operation, or decommissioning, that can be exploited to enable a threat.

- **Attack**: An attack is the action taken by a threat agent to exploit a vulnerability in order to realize a threat. For example, an inexpensive and easily picked front-door lock represents a vulnerability that a burglar (the threat agent) could exploit to gain unauthorized access (the threat) to your home (the asset). Attacks are often multi-step in nature and may exploit multiple vulnerabilities to achieve the desired outcome.

- **Risk**: Risk analysis within a TARA encompasses two factors:

    1. The likelihood that a threat agent will exploit a vulnerability, given their skills, resources, and the difficulty of the exploit; and
    2. The impact on your business and/or customer if the exploitation is successful.

    Returning to the home example, if it is widely known that you own a Picasso painting, have a poor-quality front-door lock, and lack a burglar alarm, the likelihood of exploitation of these vulnerabilities is high, and the resulting financial impact would be severe, making the overall risk unacceptable.

- Security Controls: Security controls are implemented to eliminate or minimize vulnerabilities and thereby eliminate or reduce associated threats. The goal is to reduce risk of exploitation to an acceptable level. For IoT devices, security controls typically require some combination of the following attributes: Confidentiality, Integrity, Authenticity, Availability, Authorization, Non-repudiation, Privacy, Freshness, and Trust. In the TARA process, these attributes are used both to understand the nature of the threats and to determine the appropriate controls required to mitigate them.

Security Attributes Used as Controls

The following security attributes form the foundation of effective security controls:

- **Confidentiality**: Confidentiality ensures that information is not disclosed to unauthorized entities. Unauthorized entities may include other processes within a device, external servers, individuals, or organizations. Not all data requires confidentiality; therefore, secure systems must classify data based on its confidentiality and authenticity requirements.
- **Integrity**: Integrity ensures that data has not been modified, but it does not guarantee that the data is authentic or trustworthy. For example, many communications and storage systems rely on Cyclic Redundancy Codes (CRCs) to detect accidental errors. While CRCs are effective for error detection, it is trivial to construct different messages that produce the same CRC value. As a result, CRCs alone cannot detect deliberate message substitution. For a secure product, integrity intersects with authenticity. It is necessary for the integrity mechanism to ensure that a message has not been substituted or manipulated either by a threat actor or accident. It is also necessary to know that the message was sent by an authorized participant. In this application, integrity is instead established using Message Authentication Codes (MACs) or digital signatures, both of which will be discussed later. Integrity also includes data completeness, which is especially critical for safety-related functions. For example, if a medical infusion pump receives an incomplete software update, it should transition to a safe, inoperative state rather than operate with incomplete parameters.

- **Authenticity**: Authenticity is defined in ISO 27000 as the property that an entity is what it claims to be. An authentic entity is worthy of trust and has an undisputed origin. In secure systems, authenticity applies to messages, identities, and sometimes hardware components. Authentic messages are received exactly as intended and have not been altered in transit. Authentic identities may refer to human users, devices, software processes, or even the provenance of system components. Not all elements require authentication, but it is essential to clearly identify which elements are trusted. Assuming authenticity without proof is a common source of vulnerabilities.

- **Availability**: Availability ensures that systems and assets are accessible to authorized users when needed. This attribute is particularly important in safety-critical systems, where loss of availability may create hazardous conditions. For example, loss of steering control in a drive-by-wire vehicle would pose an immediate safety risk. Similarly, if an attacker can easily jam (make unavailable) the Wi-Fi connection of a home security camera, the system will fail to record evidence of an intrusion.

- **Authorization**: Authorization is the permission granted to an entity to access a system resource. It is an access control property typically comprised of four elements:

    - the assets being protected (e.g., safety-critical calibration data),
    - the permitted actions (e.g., read or write access),
    - the authorized entities (users, organizations, processes, roles, or policies), and
    - the duration for which access is permitted.

- **Non-repudiation**: Non-repudiation prevents a message originator from later denying authorship and may also provide proof of receipt so that the recipient cannot deny delivery. When properly implemented, non-repudiation enables strong auditability. This is especially valuable in e-commerce transactions and OTA update systems. For example, if a vehicle owner approves or rejects a software update, non-repudiation provides evidence of that decision, helping to mitigate liability.

- **Privacy**: Privacy is an aspect of confidentiality that protects the relationship between data and an individual or entity from disclosure. For example, privacy ensures that unauthorized parties cannot link an individual's identity to their electronic medical records.

- **Freshness**: Freshness is a critical property that ensures information is not reused or replayed. In a financial transaction, freshness prevents an attacker from replaying a wire transfer request to extract additional funds. Freshness is typically achieved using cryptographically protected timestamps or sequence numbers.

- **Trust**: Trust is the ability to have confidence in the correct operation of a system or system component. Trusted systems rely on immutable hardware trust anchors with multiple layers of protection to safeguard sensitive data and operations. In IoT devices, trust anchors are often implemented using specialized secure microcontrollers or secure elements. In server environments, hardware security modules (HSMs) housed in protected facilities typically provide this functionality. These trust anchors will be discussed further in the next chapter.

Performing the TARA

To perform the Threat and Risk Analysis (TARA) in a structured and logical manner, we recommend using the HEAVENS risk assessment framework. HEAVENS guides the identification of threats, the assessment of their feasibility of exploitation through underlying vulnerabilities, the rating of impacts resulting from successful attacks, and the evaluation of the resulting risks.

By ranking these risks, development teams can prioritize the security controls that must be specified in the product's security architecture to mitigate them. Some of these controls will need to be implemented directly within the product's hardware and software, while others may be implemented at the enterprise or operational level.

HEAVENS Background

The HEAVENS framework was developed by the automotive industry to address vehicle cybersecurity (See Bibliography). Among the many available risk assessment frameworks, HEAVENS specifically was developed for embedded environments and it supports the assessment of both security and safety risks. As a result, it is broadly applicable to embedded and IoT devices and services, including vehicles, medical devices, and industrial control systems.

So how can this framework be applied to your products? To answer that, we begin by examining a diagram that illustrates the HEAVENS-based TARA process.

Figure 5: **The HEAVENS Process**

The HEAVENS process begins by identifying the stakeholders who may be impacted by a successful attack against the product. At the highest level, stakeholders typically include the product manufacturer, the product owner, and the product user. Each of these broad categories may contain multiple subgroups. For example, within the product manufacturer, stakeholders may include finance, legal, marketing, manufacturing, and support operations.

The product owner and product operator may be the same entity, such as the owner and driver of a personal vehicle, or they may be distinct, as in the case of an army (owner) and a soldier (operator). Identifying stakeholders enables the specification of the business and operational requirements that a product or service must meet. These requirements may be financial in nature for the company or safety-related for both the company and the customer.

Informed by, but distinct from, stakeholder requirements are the functional use cases that the product itself must support. For example, a product may need to receive near-continuous temperature sensor readings, accept periodic over-the-air (OTA) software updates, or allow a specific feature to be remotely enabled once the customer has paid for it. Use cases also encompass operational behaviors, such as waking from a power cycle into a known safe state or receiving sensor data and acting upon it.

Product use cases must also address maintenance and end-of-life considerations. For instance, when a module is replaced, possibly by a third party, the system must be able to determine whether the new component is authentic. End-of-life issues include the secure erasure of sensitive data from the product and compliance with any applicable consumer or user rights.

Once stakeholder requirements and use cases are identified, overarching security objectives can be associated with them. These objectives typically include trust, safety, financial protection, operational continuity and reliability, privacy, and regulatory compliance. For example, a medical device must ensure that its firmware, hardware, and sensors are authentic and trustworthy. It must protect patient safety by avoiding entry into dangerous or undefined states, comply with applicable FDA regulations, and safeguard patient privacy. From a business perspective, the manufacturer's revenue may depend on ensuring that only authorized and calibrated sensors can be used with the device.

The collection of use cases enables identification of the associated critical assets and their required security attributes. For example, an OTA update use case will involve critical assets such as operator identities, server identities, target device identities, cryptographic signing and encryption keys, firmware manifests, and the firmware image itself. The associated security attributes will include, at a minimum, confidentiality, integrity, authenticity, authorization, and freshness. Securing these use cases also drives cybersecurity requirements for the supporting infrastructure, including trusted execution, secure storage, and availability. These hardware and software requirements are discussed in subsequent chapters.

For each critical asset, the HEAVENS workflow requires identification of the threats and vulnerabilities affecting that asset, the attacker capabilities needed to exploit those vulnerabilities, and the mitigating security controls that already exist. Evaluating these factors results in an estimated risk level, quantified as a Security Level. If the assessed risk is unacceptable, additional security controls must be specified and applied (see Figure 5).

To systematically identify and analyze threats against critical assets, the HEAVENS process leverages the Microsoft STRIDE framework. STRIDE categorizes threats as follows:

- Spoofing of Identity,
- Tampering with Data,
- Repudiation,
- Information Disclosure,
- Denial of Service, and
- Elevation of Privilege.

Together, these categories encompass virtually all classes of cybersecurity threats, making STRIDE a compact and effective representation of the threat universe.

The STRIDE threat categories are described below.

Spoofing of Identity

Originally this was defined by Microsoft as the spoofing of user identity in which an attacker obtained legitimate credentials or authentication material in order to impersonate an authorized user. Today, the definition extends beyond human users to include digital identities used to authenticate APIs, AI agents, system processes, and devices. An attacker who acquires valid authentication or permission tokens can broadly compromise products and services. This category also includes attacks that exploit a lack of freshness, such as replaying previously valid authentication information. Additionally, it covers scenarios in which a firmware signature algorithm or signing key is compromised, causing an IoT device to accept and install unauthorized code that appears legitimate.

Tampering with Data

In this threat category, an attacker alters system data, compromising its integrity, with or without the knowledge of the system owner. Examples include modification of firmware, calibration data, OTA update payloads, or the injection of ransomware. This category also includes physical attacks on devices to extract sensitive information, such as cryptographic keys.

Repudiation

Repudiation refers to the ability of an attacker to perform unauthorized or malicious actions without traceability or attribution. Examples include undetected modification of audit logs or the initiation or replay of transactions or commands in a way that cannot later be proven.

Information Disclosure

Information disclosure threats expose corporate, product, or personal data to unauthorized parties. Recent examples include nation-state actors' exfiltrating sensitive defense designs, cybercriminals stealing healthcare records or social security numbers, or attackers obtaining code-signing keys. Some nation-states are also known to collect vast quantities of encrypted communications with the expectation that future advances in cryptanalysis will allow decryption.

Denial of Service (DoS)

In a denial-of-service attack, the attacker seeks to disrupt or degrade the availability of a product or service. Common examples include hijacking consumer IoT devices to form botnets that overwhelm online services with traffic, preventing them from responding to legitimate requests. DoS attacks may also involve sending malformed or malicious commands or data to cause devices or services to crash.

Elevation of Privilege

This threat occurs when an attacker gains unauthorized privileged access to a product or service. With elevated privileges, the attacker may exfiltrate or modify sensitive data, install malware, or otherwise compromise system operation. Elevation of privilege may be achieved through stolen credentials or by exploiting software flaws that cause a system to execute malicious commands.

Threat and Vulnerability Identification

The Threat Analysis and Risk Assessment (TARA) commences with an examination of the critical assets, product use cases, and any available implementation specifications in order to identify the STRIDE threats and vulnerabilities applicable to the planned implementation relative to these threat categories. This is a critical step in the TARA process as failure to comprehensively identify vulnerabilities can result in an incomplete or inadequate security architecture specification. Use cases are especially important in this process because, if the product relies on corporate IT services for part or all of its functionality, or on a third-party contract manufacturer for assembly, the cybersecurity of those associated systems must also be analyzed.

Adversaries will exploit any attack vector that can be discovered. Hacking relies heavily on human creativity, which is why new exploits are continuously being identified. Today, this creativity is now increasingly augmented by artificial intelligence. In addition, outsourcing elements of product development, manufacturing, and support introduces new attack paths, as third-party systems and processes expand the overall attack surface.

Depending on the stage of product development at which it is performed, the TARA may need to be revisited as implementation details become further specified. For example, during the early stages of the development cycle, when only high-level product use cases are known, threats, vulnerabilities, and security attributes can generally be identified only at a coarse level. For example, to counter user account compromise (a threat) resulting from weak passwords (a vulnerability), multifactor authentication might be specified to protect the IT infrastructure associated with the software development environment.

As the product becomes more fully specified and developed – such as when candidate microprocessors are selected, the operating system is defined, communication protocols with supporting systems and sensors are identified, and the development environment and open source components are finalized – threats and vulnerabilities can be identified with greater precision and detail. For example, the product's digital identity private key must be protected against physical compromise to prevent device cloning. Note there is not necessarily a one-to-one relationship between threats and vulnerabilities, as a single threat may exploit multiple vulnerabilities, and a single vulnerability may be exploited by multiple threats.

Commencing the Security Architecture Specification

Due to the evolving nature of the product's design and associated specifications, it is likely that the TARA will be performed or revisited multiple times, typically during the following stages: (1) the concept phase; (2) the top-level engineering specification phase; and (3) the fully specified phase, when all hardware and software design documentation is complete and the manufacturing process is defined.

The Risk Assessment

With vulnerabilities and threats identified, the next step is to assess risk. This is accomplished by evaluating the attackers' capabilities and resources, estimating the impact of a successful attack, and assigning a criticality level to each threat. Specifically, this assessment considers the attackers' expertise, their knowledge of the product and its supporting systems, the window of opportunity available to mount an attack, and the nature of the equipment required to execute it. These factors are collectively captured by the HEAVENS Threat Level Parameters.

The impact of a successful attack is then analyzed across safety, financial, operational, and privacy or compliance dimensions, collectively referred to as the Impact Level Parameters. Finally, the likelihood of a threat being realized is combined with the estimated impact to derive the HEAVENS Security Level rating. This rating enables threats to be prioritized according to their criticality and is subsequently used to determine the security controls required to reduce the risk to an acceptable level.

Threat Level Parameters

HEAVENS defines four categories of Threat Level Parameters: **Expertise**, **Knowledge of the Target of Evaluation**, **Equipment**, and

Window of Opportunity. These parameters are applied to the threat–asset pairs identified earlier in the TARA process.

Expertise

Expertise represents the level of technical skill required to execute a threat. HEAVENS defines four levels of attacker expertise:

- **Layman:** A layman can use a personal computer and standard applications but has no programming or electrical engineering skills.
- **Proficient:** A proficient attacker may be familiar with the use or maintenance of the product. Such an attacker can perform mechanical operations, such as removing and replacing components, and can make standard electrical connections, including accessing system buses or network interfaces and running protocol analyzers. A proficient attacker can execute exploits developed by others but cannot develop original exploits.
- **Expert:** An expert attacker is capable of developing exploits, including reverse-engineering executable code and writing targeted attack software. While they may not be familiar with every aspect of the system, they possess sufficient expertise to create exploits within their domain.
- **Multiple-Expert:** This level applies to attacks requiring the coordinated skills of multiple experts across different disciplines. An example would be a team consisting of a cryptanalyst, software developer, electrical engineer, and test engineer.

Knowledge of the Target of Evaluation

This parameter describes the level of knowledge required to carry out an attack against the product, referred to as the Target of Evaluation (TOE) in Common Criteria terminology. This parameter is independent of the number of attackers involved.

- **Public:** Publicly available information, including material obtainable through open sources or reverse engineering of the product.
- **Restricted:** Proprietary information with limited distribution, such as service manuals, internal technical documentation, or information shared with partners under non-disclosure agreements.
- **Sensitive:** Information with restricted access even within the organization, including design data, calibration parameters, and message formats, and database schemas.
- **Critical:** Highly protected information whose disclosure could cause severe damage, typically limited to cryptographic keys. Compromise of critical information can enable attacks against an entire class of products.

Equipment

HEAVENS defines four levels of equipment sophistication required to execute an exploit:

- **Standard:** Commonly available equipment such as personal computers, general-purpose test equipment, and widely available software tools. Examples include automotive CAN bus tools and TCP/IP network sniffers.

- **Specialized:** Equipment designed for specific tasks that is generally available but may be costly. Examples include software-defined radios, Wi-Fi hacking tools, and large server clusters used for password cracking.
- **Bespoke:** Custom-designed equipment created for a specific attack. This category includes custom software exploits and specialized tools for side-channel analysis, such as differential power analysis or RF emissions analysis.
- **Multiple-Bespoke:** Attacks that require more than one type of bespoke equipment.

Window of Opportunity

The window of opportunity describes the amount of time during which a threat is exposed and can be exploited. The longer the exposure, the greater the risk.

HEAVENS defines four levels:

- **Low:** Threats that are exposed only briefly or which require direct physical access to the product are classified as having a low window of opportunity.
- **Medium:** Threats requiring limited or temporary physical access, such as access to unlocked spaces or short-duration exposure.
- **High:** Threats that allow remote access for a limited period of time.
- **Critical:** Threats that permit continuous remote access, 24/7, over an untrusted network.

To apply these Threat Level Parameters, numerical values are assigned to each level, as defined in Table 3.

Parameter	Value
Expertise	
Layman	0
Proficient	1
Expert	2
Multiple Experts	3
Knowledge about TOE	
Public	0
Restricted	1
Sensitive	2
Critical	3
Window of Opportunity	
Critical	0
High	1
Medium	2
Low	3
Equipment	
Standard	0
Specialized	1
Bespoke	2
Multiple Bespoke	3

Table 3: **Threat Level Parameters**

The values for each parameter are summed and then assigned an overall Threat Level (TL) for the asset-threat pair per Table 4:

Total of TL Parameters	Threat Level	TL Value
> 9	None	0
7 - 9	Low	1
4 - 6	Medium	2
2 - 3	High	3
0 - 1	Critical	4

Table 4: **Estimated Overall Threat Level**

Thus, an attack against an asset that requires no specialized knowledge (**Layman, 0**), relies only on publicly available information (**Public, 0**), has an unrestricted window of opportunity (**Critical, 0**), and uses only standard equipment (**Standard, 0**) results in a **Threat Level of Critical** and a **Threat Level (TL) Value of 4**.

Impact Level Parameters

The HEAVENS framework defines four Impact Level Parameters. Impact levels are given significantly greater weight within the HEAVENS system, as reflected by severity ratings that increase by powers of ten at each successive level.

Safety Impact

In the original HEAVENS methodology, this parameter focused primarily on vehicle safety. For the purposes of this book, safety impact estimates should encompass any threat to human life resulting from an attack on the product. Assessing safety impact requires a deep understanding of potential failure modes and their consequences.

Safety impact is largely determined by the industry in which the product is deployed. As discussed previously, the HEAVENS approach is closely aligned with the ISO 26262 functional safety standard for automotive systems. However, the methodology can be readily extended to other domains, including industrial control systems, aviation, and medical devices, among others. It is also acknowledged that safety impact may not be applicable to all products.

HEAVENS assigns the following values to safety impact outcomes:

Safety Impact	Value
No Injury	0
Light to Moderate Injuries	10
Severe and life-threatening injuries but survivable	100
Life-threatening injuries with uncertain outcome, deaths	1000

Table 5: **Safety Impact Level Parameters**

Financial Impact

Financial impact should be evaluated in consultation with the finance department and those responsible for corporate insurance coverage. In most cases, threats are considered to have a high financial impact if they can significantly damage the company's brand or reputation, cause substantial revenue loss, and/or require remediation of products already shipped to customers. If a threat necessitates remediation across all deployed products, it should be rated **Very High**.

HEAVENS defines the following financial impact levels:

- **No Impact**: No financial impact.
- **Low**: Financial damage is tolerable to the organization.
- **Medium**: Financial damage results in substantial losses but does not threaten the organization's existence.
- **High**: Financial losses threaten the continued existence of the organization.

Financial Impact	Value
No Impact	0
Low	10
Medium	100
High	1000

Table 6: **Financial Impact Parameters**

HEAVENS states that this table represents one possible prioritization of damage categories. Management should review these weightings and determine whether they are appropriate for the organization's specific business context.

Operational Impact

This parameter captures the effect on organizational operations resulting from a successful attack against an asset. HEAVENS defines four levels of operational impact:

- **No Impact**: No discernible effect on operations.
- **Low**: Minor to moderate operational disruption.
- **Medium**: Moderate to significant disruption (e.g., degradation of a primary function).
- **High**: Major disruption (e.g., loss of a primary function, physical damage to attached equipment, or failure to meet safety or regulatory requirements).

Weightings for the operational impact parameters are shown in Table 7.

Operational Impact	Value
No Effect	0
Low	1
Medium	10
High	100

Table 7: **Operational Impact Parameters**

Privacy and Compliance

The final impact parameter combines the effects of private information disclosure and violations of law. HEAVENS uses the term *legal*; however, the more accurate term is *compliance*. *Legal* refers strictly to matters of law, whereas *compliance* encompasses adherence to, or violation of, laws, regulations, and contractual obligations. As such, *compliance* more accurately captures the scope of this impact category.

HEAVENS defines the following four levels for privacy and compliance impact:

- **No Impact**: No disclosure of private information or no violations of law or regulation.
- **Low**: Disclosure of private information relating to a single stakeholder that is unlikely to lead to abuse. Violations of law or regulation without appreciable consequences.
- **Medium**: Disclosure of private information relating to a single stakeholder that leads to abuse. Violations of law or regulation with potential consequences for business operations or finances.
- **High**: Disclosure of private information relating to multiple stakeholders leading to abuses. Violations of law or regulation resulting in significant consequences for business operations or finances.

The weightings for these impact parameters are shown in the following table.

Privacy & Compliance	Value	Explanation
No Impact	0	
Low	1	Privacy violation for an individual (or group) but not leading to other abuses such as identity theft; compliance failure, but without appreciable consequences
Medium	10	Privacy violation for one or more stakeholders with subsequent impacts to them; results in media coverage; financial consequences are tolerable
High	100	Privacy violation for many stakeholders with subsequent abuses; significant media coverage; significant penalties and other consequences

Table 8: **Privacy & Compliance Impact Parameters**

As a last step, all of the estimated values for the different impact parameters are summed to create a final overall Impact Level Rating which is shown in the following table:

Sum of Individual Impact Level Parameters	Overall Impact Level	Value
0	No Impact	0
1 – 19	Low	1
20 -99	Medium	2
100 – 999	High	3
≥1000	Critical	4

Table 9: **Estimated Overall Impact Level Rating**

Security Level

This is the final step in the HEAVENS TARA process in which the relationship between the totals for the overall Threat Level and the overall Impact Level are ranked to determine the criticality of a successful Threat.

Security Level	Impact Level					
Threat Level		0	1	2	3	4
	0	QM	QM	QM	QM	Low
	1	QM	Low	Low	Low	Medium
	2	QM	Low	Medium	Medium	High
	3	QM	Low	Medium	High	High
	4	Low	Medium	High	High	Critical

Table 10: **Security Level Rating**

In Table 10, the lowest Security Level is identified as **"QM"**, which stands for *Quality Management*. This designation indicates that the associated risk can be addressed through standard practices such as employee training, established procedures, or product documentation. As shown in the table, a Security Level of **"Critical"** should be rare and represents a severe issue for both the product and the organization. A **Security Level of "High"** should also be treated as a serious concern.

Some debate should be expected around **"Medium"** Security Levels and whether remediation is required. However, we recommend that as many *Medium*-level risks as possible be remediated, with the goal of achieving an overall product Security Level of **"Low/QM."** Risks at these levels are typically of limited consequence or may be partially mitigated through organizational controls or insurance coverage.

The TARA process should not be given short shrift. It requires focused analysis and can be difficult and, at times, frustrating, as it relies as much on expert judgment and experience as on hard data. While risk levels associated with specific threat–vulnerability pairs may be subject to prolonged debate, we encourage teams to place a proverbial *"stake in the ground"* using conservative assumptions that reflect higher-risk scenarios. Given that threats may originate from a wide spectrum of attackers, exploiting weaknesses in corporate IT infrastructure, third-party systems, or the design and operation of the IoT device itself, a multidisciplinary analysis team is essential.

As an example of the TARA process, consider an Industrial Control System (ICS) used to manage an oil production field. For this illustration, we remain at a high level and examine only a limited set of threats. In this scenario, the ICS manufacturer's customer is a petroleum company. The fictional company's control network is shown in Figure 6.

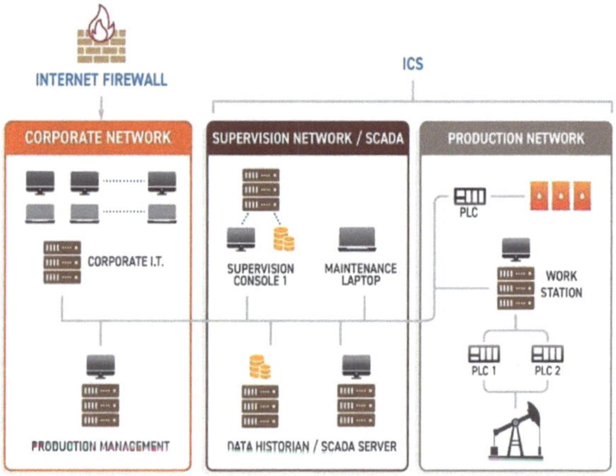

Figure 6: **Fictional Petroleum Company's Network**

Critical Assets

- Control logic used by the PLC to operate the oil field
- User login credentials for workstations and remote access
- PLC platform authenticity and availability

Identified Vulnerabilities

- Control logic downloads are not authenticated
- Supervision Console control-logic programming software and local data files are not protected against modification
- Weak passwords in the IT environment; default passwords on PLCs are never changed

Threat Agents

- Hacker
- Disgruntled Employee
- Organized Crime
- Nation-State

Motivation

These threat agents are interested in disrupting the company's production services, whether for notoriety, revenge, political statement, or preparation for future cyber warfare activities.

Resources

A hacker or disgruntled employee is likely to have limited technical capabilities but may leverage legitimate or stolen employee IT credentials. A nation-state attacker, by contrast, will have significant technical and financial resources, including the ability to purchase identical ICS equipment for detailed analysis and exploit development.

Vulnerability (Attack Vector)

The OT/ICS network is connected to the enterprise IT network which in turn is connected to the internet. An attacker gains access to the enterprise-connected Supervision Console platform and PLC devices, authenticates using embedded default credentials, and reconfigures control logic and system settings.

STRIDE Classification

- Tampering
- Elevation of Privilege
- Spoofing
- Denial of Service

Attackers are able to access the systems, move laterally within the OT network, alter decision logic, and rename devices such that they can no longer be controlled. This leads to pump shutdowns and loss of control over field pipelines and storage tanks.

HEAVENS Threat Level: High (Overall Rating: 3)

- **Expertise:** Expert (2)
- **Knowledge of the Target of Evaluation:** Restricted (1)

  The attacker begins with owner documentation and publicly available service manuals and incrementally develops deeper system knowledge.

- **Window of Opportunity:** Critical (0)

  The attacker has continuous access to internet-connected devices and does not require a specialized exploit.

- **Equipment:** Standard (0)

  The attack uses readily available software tools.

HEAVENS Impact Level: High (Overall Rating: 3)

Commencing the Security Architecture Specification

- **Safety Impact:** No injury (0)
- **Financial Impact:** High (100)

  The attack impacts a large oil field. System restart is slow, and a potential oil spill would trigger regulatory oversight requiring significant executive involvement. Government agencies and surrounding communities may pursue legal action, and brand damage would be substantial.

- **Operational Impact:** High (8)

  Major disruption of production services with downstream impacts to customers.

- **Privacy & Compliance Impact:** Medium (10)

  Violation of standard IT cybersecurity due-care requirements; violation of environmental regulations; regulators may impose financial penalties.

Overall HEAVENS Security Level: High

Security Requirements

With the Security Level determined for each critical asset, the Security Requirements can now be specified. This phase consists of identifying the appropriate security attributes to protect each critical asset based on the identified threat(s) to them. These results will be used in the development of the Security Architecture Specification in which the appropriate cryptosystems, protocols, software, hardware, policies and procedures are identified to protect the product throughout its lifecycle.

Using the prior simple example, Table 11 shows how security requirements are specified and mapped during this step.

Asset Name	Asset Type	Asset Location	Asset Owner	Asset Lifetime	Asset Security Attribute	Security Level
PLC Firmware Image	Data	Third-party Manufacturing Server, PLC	OEM	30 yrs	Confidentiality, Integrity, Authenticity,	Medium
Firmware Update	Data	Update Server, PLC	OEM	30 years	Confidentiality, Integrity, Authenticity, Freshness, Authorization	Critical
Control Logic	Data	PLC	Customer	30 years	Integrity, Authenticity,	High
PLC	Hardware	Field	Customer	30 years	Integrity, Authenticity, Availability	High
Production Network Engineering Workstation	Hardware/Control Logic Application/Data	Operations	Customer	30 years	Integrity, Authenticity, Authorization, Availability	High
Supervision Control Console	Hardware/Control Logic Application/Data	Operations	Customer	30 years	Integrity, Authenticity, Authorization, Availability	High

Table11: ***Security Requirements for Petroleum Company Example***

As the TARA process highlights, the critical assets on which an IoT device relies can be attacked at multiple points throughout its lifecycle. When viewed across the product lifecycle, as illustrated in Figure 7, it becomes clear that TARA-driven security requirements extend beyond the device itself to encompass all related systems, services, policies, and procedures that interact with the product.

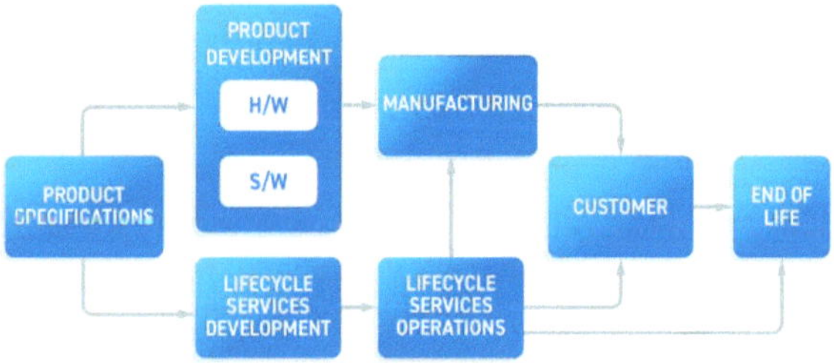

Figure 7: **The Product Lifecycle**

Starting with product development, there are multiple touchpoints to consider. For example, portions of development may be outsourced to third parties. Does your team have detailed knowledge of those vendors' development environments and the open-source software they use to create the product or supporting services? Do your coding standards, and theirs, explicitly address the development of secure software? Have your product development and IT teams addressed the security and availability of required support services, such as cloud storage or over-the-air (OTA) updates? Does the selected CPU provide the necessary security functionality to meet the TARA-derived security requirements?

Once the product moves into manufacturing, how will critical assets be protected on a third-party manufacturing line (or on your own, for that matter)? Assets must not be stolen, misused, or misconfigured during this phase. After the product is sold, it will remain in operation until its end-of-life (EOL). For most consumer products, EOL simply involves disposal. However, for high-value products containing sensitive data—such as laptops with persistent storage, ICS processing logic and data, or autonomous driving firmware—secure data erasure may be required, and the product may need to be electronically disabled.

By following this structured TARA process, the resulting detailed security requirements, implemented in both the product and its ecosystem's hardware and software, can be traced back to the initial, high-level security requirements, demonstrating full coverage of the TARA's findings. How these security requirements are implemented across the product lifecycle is the subject of the next chapter.

IoT security must be built in, automatic, and cost-effective. Given the scale and volume of deployed devices, reliance on human intervention for cybersecurity must be minimized. It should be clear that reducing the attack surface during the design phase is far more effective than attempting to remediate security weaknesses after the product has been deployed. This is the primary objective of the Security Architecture Specification.

Translating Security Requirements to Reality

Or How I Learned to Love Cryptography

To realize the TARA-derived security requirements in the embedded device and its associated services, we turn to the field of cryptography. When properly implemented, cryptography enables trust in products and their operation. Cryptography is directly related to the HEAVENS analysis because it is the primary technology used to provide the core security properties of critical assets: confidentiality, integrity, and authenticity.

This chapter begins with a cryptography primer to provide essential background, followed by a discussion of the implementation choices required for defining a detailed Cybersecurity Concept. This concept guides engineering, manufacturing, and operational teams in the design, manufacture, and deployment of an IoT product. This chapter is grounded in real-world experience implementing cybersecurity requirements across the full product lifecycle.

A Cryptography Primer

Cryptography is the science of encoding and decoding data so that it is unintelligible to unauthorized parties and/or cannot be modified without detection. In modern digital systems, the properties of authenticity, confidentiality, and non-repudiation are established and proven through cryptographic techniques. Any specification for secure digital systems must therefore begin with an understanding of fundamental cryptographic functions.

In this primer, we reference only algorithms approved by recognized standards bodies, such as the U.S. National Institute of Standards and Technology (NIST), the Internet Engineering Task Force (IETF), and the International Organization for Standardization (ISO), as these represent best practices and provide organizations with a strong technical and regulatory justification for their use.

Kerckhoffs's Principle

Modern cryptography relies extensively on standardized algorithms that are public and widely available. As a result, the security of a cryptographic system cannot depend on the secrecy of the algorithm itself. Instead, security must rely solely on the confidentiality of the associated secret keys. This concept, known as **Kerckhoffs's Principle**, was first articulated in the 19th century by Dutch cryptographer Auguste Kerckhoffs.

This principle has two important real-world implications. First, system designers must assume that attackers are fully aware of the algorithms and implementation methods being used. History has shown that attackers are remarkably effective at uncovering so-called "secret" or proprietary algorithms. Hence the well-known maxim in cryptography: *there is no security through obscurity.*

Second, the security of the entire system depends on the protection of the cryptographic keys. Compromise of a key places every entity that depends on that key at risk. This leads to an important system design principle: wherever possible, the impact of a key compromise should be limited. As a result, cryptographic systems are typically designed using hierarchical key structures, where higher-level keys are afforded greater protection than lower-level keys.

Higher-level keys protect a broader set of assets and therefore require stronger safeguards. For example, the compromise of a private key associated with a single vehicle affects only that vehicle, whereas compromise of an OEM's root certificate authority (CA) private key would undermine the security of every vehicle and service protected by that root key.

Cryptographic Hash Functions

A cryptographic hash function takes as input a message of arbitrary length and produces a fixed-length output, commonly referred to as a *digest* or *hash*. A cryptographically secure hash function must possess the following properties:

- It must be computationally infeasible to find two distinct messages that produce the same hash value (*collision resistance*).
- Given only a hash value, it must be computationally infeasible to determine an input message that produces that hash (*preimage resistance*).
- Given an original message and its hash, it must be computationally infeasible to find a second message that produces the same hash (*second preimage resistance*).

In essence, hashing is a one-way function: it is easy to compute the hash from a message, but impractical to reconstruct the original message from the hash. A commonly used analogy is smashing a porcelain plate on a hard floor. Breaking the plate is easy; reconstructing the original plate from the scattered fragments is virtually impossible.

This one-way property is unique to cryptographic hash functions. Engineers with a data communications background are often familiar with error-detection codes such as Cyclic Redundancy Codes (CRCs), which are widely used to detect transmission errors. However, CRCs do not provide cryptographic security properties. In particular, it is trivial to construct multiple messages that yield the same CRC value, making CRCs unsuitable for security applications.

Cryptographic hash functions provide strong assurance of *data integrity*, but they do not provide *authenticity*. This is because anyone can compute a hash for a given message. Authenticity is established through the use of a Message Authentication Code (MAC) or a digital signature, which are discussed in the following sections.

Several cryptographic hash standards are widely used in industry today. The most prominent are the Secure Hash Algorithm (SHA) families, including SHA-2 (defined in FIPS 180-4) and SHA-3 (defined in FIPS 202). Hash functions can also be constructed from symmetric encryption algorithms, such as the Advanced Encryption Standard (AES), as specified in FIPS 197.

Message Authentication Codes

How can authenticity be assured for a message? Message Authentication Codes (MACs) provide authenticity by incorporating a shared secret key, known only to the sender and receiver, into the computation of a cryptographic hash. The resulting output is referred to as a MAC.

To generate a MAC, the sender combines the message with the shared secret key and computes a cryptographic hash over the combined data. The sender then transmits both the message and the MAC, but never the key itself. Upon receipt, the receiver uses their copy of the shared secret key to compute a MAC over the received message. If the computed MAC matches the received MAC, the receiver can be confident that the message was generated by an entity in possession of the shared secret key and that the message has not been modified in transit.

If the secret key is shared among multiple entities, the receiver can verify that the message originated from one of the authorized key holders, but cannot determine precisely which one sent it.

A widely used MAC construction is HMAC, specified in FIPS 198-1 and NIST SP 800-224, and commonly implemented using either the SHA-2 or SHA-3 hash families. Symmetric encryption algorithms such as AES can also be used to generate MACs, as defined in the NIST SP 800-38 series.

Symmetric Key Cryptography

Symmetric key cryptography provides the security attribute of *confidentiality*. It is termed *symmetric* because the same secret key is used to both encrypt and decrypt a message. A common analogy is the key to the front door of a home: the same key is used to lock and unlock the door. Unlike a physical door key, however, a cryptographic key is a random (or pseudorandom) bit string used to parameterize the encryption algorithm.

Symmetric key algorithms are significantly more computationally efficient than public key algorithms (discussed later). As a result, they are the preferred choice for high-speed, low latency encryption and for protecting large volumes of data.

There are three classes of symmetric key cryptosystems: block ciphers, stream ciphers, and one-time pads. Of these, block ciphers dominate most commercial cryptographic systems. Stream ciphers are typically used in scenarios involving continuous data streams rather than discrete, structured messages and are supported by fewer widely adopted standards. One-time pads, while theoretically providing perfect secrecy, require key material that is as long as the plaintext message and must never be reused. These requirements render them impractical for most real-world applications.

Accordingly, this book focuses on block ciphers as the symmetric cryptosystem of choice.

A block cipher operates by transforming a fixed-size block of plaintext (unencrypted data) into a corresponding block of ciphertext (encrypted data). Typical block sizes range from 8 bytes to 32 bytes. The most widely deployed block cipher today is the Advanced Encryption Standard (AES), which has a fixed block size of 128 bits and supports key lengths of 128, 192, or 256 bits.

Block Cipher Modes of Operation

Because block ciphers operate only on fixed-length blocks of data, additional mechanisms are required to encrypt messages longer than a single block. These mechanisms are known collectively as *block cipher modes of operation*.

The simplest mode of operation encrypts each block of plaintext independently using the same key. This mode is known as Electronic Codebook (ECB) mode. ECB has a critical weakness: identical plaintext blocks always produce identical ciphertext blocks when encrypted with the same key. This property can leak information about the structure of the plaintext and may allow an attacker to infer sensitive details.

Figure 8 illustrates this weakness. Due to its deterministic nature, ECB is generally reserved for encrypting pseudorandom data, such as cryptographic keys.

Figure 8: **Block Cipher Modes of Operation**

There are several additional block cipher modes of operation, including Cipher Block Chaining (CBC), Cipher Feedback (CFB), Counter Mode (CTR), and Galois/Counter Mode (GCM), among others. Selection of the appropriate mode depends on the application and its security requirements. The NIST SP 800-38 series provides authoritative guidance on the selection and correct use of these modes.

In many cases, the mode of operation is dictated by the application or protocol itself. Modern cryptographic protocols, such as IPsec and Transport Layer Security (TLS), specify approved encryption modes. However, care must still be taken in selecting which of the approved modes is most appropriate, as not all modes provide the same security properties.

The Key Distribution Problem

As previously described, symmetric key cryptography requires that the sender and receiver securely share a secret key in order to communicate. The process of establishing this shared secret is known as *key distribution*. If the communicating parties know each other and are co-located, keys might be exchanged manually and in person. However, this approach does not scale to systems in which counterparties are unknown in advance or separated by significant distances.

Consider the complexity of key distribution in a network of 1,000 interconnected IoT devices, where each device must communicate securely with every other device. In such a fully connected network, approximately 500,000 individual key exchange relationships would be required. Clearly, this approach is infeasible.

In the early days of cryptography, prior to the 1980s, the military distributed cryptographic keys using punched paper tape transported by armed courier. Commercial organizations similarly relied on couriers or tamper-evident packaging to distribute keys. This approach, known as *manual key distribution*, was slow, expensive, and error-prone. More importantly, it was entirely incompatible with the scale and speed of modern digital networks.

The John Walker Espionage Case

The demise of manual key distribution within the military was accelerated by one of the most damaging espionage cases in U.S. history: that of John Walker.

John Walker served in the U.S. Navy from 1967 to 1976. During this period, symmetric keys used by most U.S. encryption devices were stored on paper key cards, with the key material physically punched into the card. These cards were inserted into encryption devices to load the active keys. Walker exploited his access to this keying material by photocopying or photographing the cards and selling the information to the Soviet Union. Financially motivated, Walker earned approximately $4,000 per month from Soviet intelligence while his Navy salary was only $480 per month.

In 1968, shortly after Walker began spying, North Korea seized the USS *Pueblo*, reportedly at Soviet request, in order to obtain a KW-7 encryptor. The KW-7 was the most widely deployed encryption device in the U.S. military, as well as within the CIA and NATO. Many of the compromised keys provided by Walker were used by this device. Walker also supplied the Soviets with the operational and maintenance manuals for the KW-7.

While serving on earlier ships, Walker had legitimate access only to the keying material for those specific vessels. However, the most severe compromise occurred during his service aboard the supply ship USS *Niagara Falls* from 1971 to 1974. The Navy divided the world into four operational regions, each using distinct cryptographic keys for surface ships, submarines, aircraft, and other assets. Because ships frequently moved between regions, they were required to interoperate with vessels in any theater.

As a supply ship, the USS *Niagara Falls* carried large volumes of keying material for all regions to support fleet operations. These keys were stored in a vault to which Walker had authorized access in his role as a Classified Material System (CMS) custodian. Walker was able to photograph this extensive collection of cryptographic keys and deliver the film to his Soviet handlers.

Later in his career, Walker recruited a friend, John Whitworth, as well as family members to expand his espionage network. When Walker was arrested in 1985, it was estimated that the Soviets had been able to decrypt more than one million classified messages from U.S. Navy surface ships and submarines. Among known espionage cases, Walker's is considered one of the most damaging to U.S. national security.

The Rise of Public Key Cryptography

Due to these practical issues and security challenges, commercial cryptography remained limited in scope until the mid-1980s. This changed with the invention of public key cryptography, which made secure, scalable, and cost-effective key management possible.

In 1976, Whitfield Diffie and Martin Hellman published the seminal paper *"New Directions in Cryptography"*, demonstrating how two parties could establish a shared secret without any prior exchange of secret information. This breakthrough showed that secrets could be derived using only publicly exchanged data, thereby eliminating the need for manual key distribution.

This innovation fundamentally solved the cost and scalability problem inherent in symmetric key systems and laid the foundation for modern secure communications. The Diffie–Hellman paper formally established the field of public key cryptography.

A conceptual illustration of how a public key cryptographic system operates is shown in Figure 9.

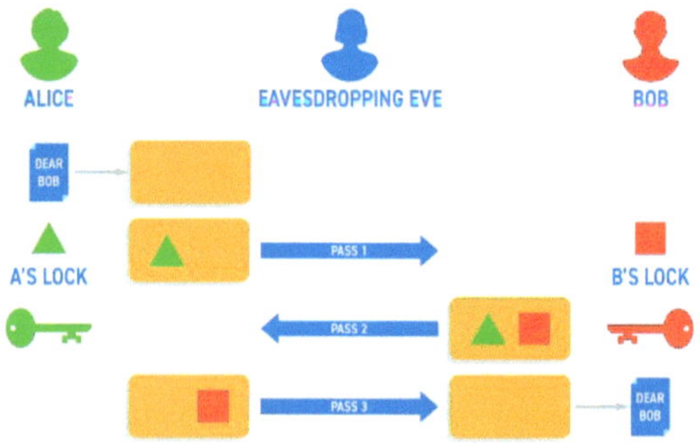

Figure 9: **3 Pass Protocol**

In this figure, Alice and Bob – the first couple of cryptography – wish to communicate securely. Each has a unique key and a padlock. Alice's key cannot unlock Bob's padlock, and Bob's key cannot unlock Alice's padlock. Alice places her message (which could, for example, be an AES key) into a lockbox, secures it with her padlock, and sends it to Bob. An eavesdropper, Eve, cannot read the message because she cannot open the lockbox.

When Bob receives the lockbox, he is unable to open it, so he adds his own padlock and sends the box back to Alice. Once again, Eve is thwarted by the locked box. When Alice receives it, she can no longer open the lockbox herself, but she removes her padlock and sends the box back to Bob. Finally, when Bob receives the lockbox, he removes his padlock and opens the box to retrieve the message.

This three-pass protocol is not efficient, but it illustrates how two parties can exchange a secret without any *a priori* exchange of other secret information.

Public key cryptographic systems have revolutionized the practice of cryptography. They solved the key distribution problem, dramatically reduced the cost and complexity of key management, strengthened authentication, and enabled non-repudiation. Three public key algorithms have been widely standardized and deployed for key exchange: Rivest–Shamir–Adleman (RSA), Diffie–Hellman (DH), and Elliptic Curve Diffie–Hellman (ECDH).

These algorithms are based on mathematical problems that are computationally infeasible for today's classical computers, which perform calculations sequentially. To prepare for the advent of quantum computers, which can operate on multiple states simultaneously, NIST has standardized a quantum-resistant public key algorithm for key establishment: FIPS 203, also known as ML-KEM.

The primary drawback of public key algorithms is that they are computationally expensive. As a result, they are typically used for key exchange and digital signatures, but not for bulk data encryption. This limitation is especially relevant for embedded and IoT devices with constrained CPU performance, memory, and power budgets, making careful algorithm selection and implementation essential.

The public key algorithms commonly used for key exchange – RSA, DH, ECDH, and ML-KEM – differ in their mathematical foundations, but at a high level they operate in similar ways. In each system, two keys are generated: a private key, which the owner keeps secret and never shares, and a public key, which isn't confidential and can be freely distributed.

These keys are mathematically related, but due to the underlying computational complexity, knowledge of the public key does not enable an attacker to derive the private key. The keys are asymmetric in the sense that when one key is used for encryption, the other must be used for decryption, and vice versa.

Public Key Transport and Key Agreement

Public key cryptography enables two users to establish a shared secret key, or to transmit a key from one party to another, without any prior exchange of secret information. This shared secret can then be used for symmetric encryption.

Using RSA, if Alice wishes to send Bob an AES-encrypted message, she first generates an AES key and encrypts her message with it. She then encrypts the AES key using Bob's public key and sends both the encrypted key and the encrypted message (ciphertext) to Bob. Since only Bob possesses the corresponding private key, he can decrypt the AES key and then use it to decrypt the message. This process is known as *key transport*.

Elliptic Curve Diffie–Hellman operates somewhat differently. Alice and Bob exchange public keys and then each applies a cryptographic operation to the received public key using their own private key. This results in both parties independently deriving the same shared secret, which can then be used as an AES key. This approach is known as *key agreement*, since neither party directly sends the key to the other. ML-KEM also functions as a key agreement mechanism.

These descriptions are intentionally high-level; many important implementation details, checks, and safeguards have been omitted for clarity.

Because a user's public key can be distributed widely, anyone can use it to encrypt a message to that user. The sender can be confident that only the intended recipient will be able to decrypt the message, since only the recipient possesses the corresponding private key. However, the recipient has no inherent assurance of the sender's identity, since anyone could have used the public key to encrypt the message. This lack of sender authentication is a critical security gap, one that we will address next.

Digital Signatures

Public key cryptography can also be used to create digital signatures, allowing one party to sign a message such that any third party can verify both its authenticity and its origin. Unlike handwritten signatures, digital signatures are intrinsically bound to the entire content of the message.

When a paper contract is signed with pen and ink, the signature alone does not guarantee that the document cannot be altered afterward. In contrast, a digitally signed document cannot be modified without detection, as any change to the content will cause signature verification to fail.

Suppose Alice wishes to send a digitally signed message to Bob. To create the signature, Alice first computes a cryptographic hash of the message, producing a message digest. She then signs this digest using her private key. The resulting value is the digital signature, which is transmitted along with the original message.

Upon receipt of the signed message, Bob first hashes the message *excluding the signature* to generate a local copy of the message digest. He then uses Alice's public key to verify the signature on the transmitted message digest. If the locally generated message digest matches the digest recovered from the signature, the authenticity and integrity of the message are verified. As before, this is a high-level description, and many important implementation details have been omitted for clarity.

RSA was the first public key scheme to be widely adopted for digital signatures. NIST standardized digital signature schemes based on RSA and the Elliptic Curve Digital Signature Algorithm (ECDSA) in FIPS 186-5. In anticipation of practical quantum computers, NIST has also standardized post-quantum digital signature algorithms, including FIPS 204 (ML-DSA) and FIPS 205 (SLH-DSA), which are designed to resist attacks by quantum-capable adversaries.

Digitally signed messages cannot be repudiated by the signer as long as the signer's private key remains confidential and the underlying algorithm remains secure against cryptanalytic attack. Under these conditions, no other party could have generated the signature. It is important to note that public keys used for digital signatures must be distinct from those used for key exchange.

Trust in Public Key Ownership

A remaining challenge for both key management and digital signatures is establishing trust in the ownership of public keys. In public key systems, Alice's and Bob's exchanged public keys must be authenticated to prevent man-in-the-middle attacks. In such an attack, an adversary (Eve) inserts herself into the communication channel and impersonates each party to the other, pretending to be Bob when communicating with Alice and pretending to be Alice when communicating with Bob. By substituting her own public keys, Eve can intercept and potentially decrypt communications without either party's knowledge.

To prevent this, digital signatures and trusted third parties are used to certify public key ownership. These mechanisms form the basis of public key infrastructure (PKI), which we will discuss in a later section.

Key and Algorithm Strength

Symmetric cryptographic algorithms are designed so that there is no more efficient way to break an encrypted message than by attempting all possible keys until the correct one is found, commonly referred to as a brute-force or exhaustion attack. If the algorithm has this property and the keys are chosen uniformly at random from the set of all possible keys (the full key space), an attacker must try, on average, half of all possible keys.

To understand the impact of bit length on the key space, consider that a symmetric algorithm with a 64-bit key has a key space of 2^{64}, or 18,446,744,073,709,551,616 possible keys. Adding just one additional bit doubles the key space. Increasing the key size to 128 bits raises the key space to 2^{128}, or approximately 3.4×10^{38} possibilities, an increase of roughly 19 orders of magnitude. Thus, a modest increase in key length can render brute-force attacks computationally infeasible.

Symmetric algorithm strength is measured in bits of key length. Two cryptographic algorithms are considered to have equivalent strength if breaking them requires approximately the same amount of computational effort, typically measured against the cost of a brute-force search of the key space.

For other types of algorithms, such as hash functions and public key cryptosystems, strength is determined by the computational effort required to break them using the best known attacks and available computing resources. If breaking a public key algorithm of a given key size requires approximately the same effort as brute-forcing a symmetric algorithm of a certain key length, the two are said to provide equivalent cryptographic strength.

Based on this concept of equivalent computational work, a security architect can select the parameters for each cryptographic algorithm used in her project so that they all provide the same minimum level of cryptographic strength. This ensures there is no proverbial weak link among any one of the different algorithms.

Because computing capabilities and cryptanalytic techniques improve over time, cryptographic strength is not static. Algorithm and key size selection must account for the expected lifetime of the information being protected. This is a critical and often overlooked reality: cryptographic security degrades over time, and implementations must plan accordingly. Examples include:

- In the late 1980s, RSA using 512 bits was considered adequate for commercial use. By the early 1990s, advances in cryptanalysis and computing power necessitated a shift to using 1024 bits.

- In 2005, NIST published guidance on selecting appropriate cryptographic algorithms (Table 12).

Estimated Security Lifetime	**Symmetric Key Algorithm**	**Hash**	**RSA**	**ECC (ECDH, ECDSA)**
Through 2010	Triple DES, AES-128, AES-256	SHA-1, SHA-2 family	1024	160
Through 2030	AES-128, AES-256	SHA-2 family	2048	224
Beyond 2030	AES-128, AES-256	SHA-2 family	3072	256

Table12: **2005 Cryptosystem Guidance**

- As of 2025, updated guidance removes certain algorithms and introduces others in anticipation of quantum computing capabilities.

Estimated Security Lifetime	**Security Strength**	**Symmetric Key Algorithm (min key size)**	**Hash (min hash size)**	**RSA**	**ECC (ECDH, ECDSA)**	**Post Quantum (ML-KEM, ML-DSA)**
Through Year 2030	128	AES-128,	SHA-256, SHA3-256	3072	256	ML-KEM-512 (2400 bits) ML-DSA-44 (10,496 bits)
	256	AES-256	SHA-512, SHA3-512	15360	512+	ML-KEM-1024 (12,544 bits) ML-DSA-87 (20,736 bits
Beyond Year 2030	128	Not Recommended	Not Recommended	Deprecated	Deprecated	ML-KEM-512 (2400 bits) ML-DSA-44 (10,496 bits)
	256	AES-256	SHA-512, SHA3-512	Deprecated	Deprecated	ML-KEM-1024 (12,544 bits) ML-DSA-87 (20,736 bits

Table13: **2025 Cryptosystem Guidance**

This table highlights how improvements in computing power and cryptanalytic research directly influence key size recommendations. Once practical quantum computers become available, widely used algorithms such as RSA and ECC are expected to become insecure. Post-quantum cryptographic algorithms, while resistant to such attacks, will impose significantly higher requirements for computation, memory, and communication bandwidth, making them particularly challenging for embedded systems.

Key Management

Cryptographic keys must be properly managed throughout their lifecycle: generation, distribution, storage, use, and destruction. This is essential to maintaining the overall security posture of the product.

Key generation relies upon high-quality random number generators (RNGs). These RNGs must be carefully designed and manufactured to avoid bias, as any limitation or predictability in randomness can significantly aid attackers. It is critical that the full entropy of the RNG be used when generating keys.

Bill Lattin recounts an example of the perils of failing to use the full random key space in key generation for the physical world of door locks:

> Many years ago, I was at the Crypto conference at UC Santa Barbara where an attendee who had studied locksmithing as a hobby said he could easily determine the master key to the rooms in a dormitory where many of us were staying. He collected maybe 5 or 6 room keys, and then he was able to analyze the cutting patterns for the door lock tumbler pins. When he found a tumbler pin cut position that had been omitted from the set of individual room keys, he knew this was reserved for the master key. Thus, he was able to go pin-by-pin and readily determine the omitted pattern thus

creating a master key – which he then proceeded to cut and successfully demonstrate!

Clearly bias and/or limitations in the key space of a key can aid the attacker. This topic will be discussed further in the section on random number generator implementation.

To further limit attacker success, devices should periodically replace cryptographic keys where feasible, a practice commonly referred to as *key rotation*, though it more accurately involves not rotating among a pre-determined set of keys, but generating new keys and securely destroying old ones. Key changes limit the risks associated with the compromise of a particular key. A key change may be triggered by time, data volume, or specific events. High-throughput systems, such as gigabit VPNs, require more frequent key changes due to increased exposure.

In some embedded systems, post-manufacturing key changes may not be possible due to connectivity or bandwidth limitations. In such cases, long-term keys must be physically protected, unique per device, and never shared. For example, symmetric keys used to control JTAG debug access should be unique to each device to prevent a single compromise from affecting an entire product line.

Long-term public key pairs, such as those used by certificate authorities, should also be periodically replaced. Techniques such as elector-based signing, where multiple independent entities validate a new key, can be used to securely distribute replacement keys. In approaching the product's cryptographic design, the default design choice should be to enable key changes whenever possible. Permanent use of key should be carefully reviewed. NIST SP 800-57 provides guidance on key usage periods.

Public key validation is essential to prevent the compromise of keys and data when using public key systems. Received public keys must be verified to ensure they are well-formed and safe for use. NIST standards provide details on these validation checks. This is not an abstract requirement. An early version of Bluetooth was compromised by the failure to require public key validation. Additionally, separate key pairs must be used for signing and key exchange, as reusing a single pair can lead to compromise.

Finally, cryptographic keys must be securely stored so they are not easily recoverable by an adversary. Depending on the threat model, this may involve anti-fuse probe-resistant one-time programmable memory, a metal layer on chip die to prevent probing, tamper-detection combined with memory erasure mechanisms, and enforced key erasure policies prior to servicing or disposal. As with physical keys, cryptographic keys must be protected against unauthorized access throughout their lifetime.

Public Key Infrastructure (PKI)

Certificate Authorities

Public key cryptography provides the tools necessary to establish strong assurances of identity, create shared secret keys, and prevent message repudiation. However, these tools alone do not establish trust. For example, while the Elliptic Curve Diffie–Hellman (ECDH) key exchange can securely derive a shared secret, it does not authenticate the identities of the communicating endpoints. Similarly, public key algorithms can provide strong proofs of identity, but only if the associated public keys are reliably published and authenticated.

This challenge is compounded by the fact that secure communications are often established between parties who have never met and have not previously exchanged information. Recall the three-pass key exchange scenario: if Eve impersonates Bob to Alice, she can return her own public key to Alice. At the conclusion of the exchange, Eve can decrypt the secret sent by Alice and then forward it to Bob by performing a separate three-pass exchange with him. In this manner, Eve successfully positions herself as a man-in-the-middle.

If Alice and Bob can each prove ownership of their respective public keys, this attack is defeated. This assurance is provided through the use of a Public Key Infrastructure (PKI), in which one or more Certificate Authorities (CAs) act as trusted third parties (TTPs) that vouch for users (subscribers) and their associated public keys.

A trusted third party is an entity whose operations are highly regulated, secure, and reliable. As a result, its subscribers and relying parties can have confidence in the statements it issues which take the form of digital certificates. A CA certifies the identity of a subscriber and verifies that the subscriber possesses a valid public/private key pair. The CA then issues a certificate—a structured data object containing the subscriber's public key, the subscriber's identity, the CA's identity, and additional metadata—which is digitally signed using the CA's private signing key.

An appropriate analogy is a national passport authority. The authority verifies an individual's identity and citizenship, then issues a difficult-to-forge document attesting to that identity. Third parties trust the statements in the passport because they trust the secure and regulated operation of the issuing authority.

Examples of commonly used certificate formats include ITU-T X.509 version 3 and IEEE 1609.2 certificates. X.509 certificates are relatively large and are widely used in enterprise and Internet-based systems. More compact certificate formats, such as IEEE

1609.2, are designed for communications-constrained embedded environments, including Vehicle-to-Vehicle (V2V) communication systems. Figure 10 illustrates the major contents of an ITU-T X.509v3 certificate.

VERSION (v3)
Certificate Serial Number
Signature Algorithm ID
Issuer Name
Validity (not before, not after times)
Subject Name
Subject Public Key (including algorithm ID)
Extensions
Issuer Signature

Figure10: **X.509v3 Certificate Contents**

A Certificate Authority (CA) also possesses its own certificate for its public key. If a CA is a standalone CA or a top-level root CA in a hierarchy, it creates a self-signed certificate. If the CA is part of a hierarchy (an intermediate or lower CA), its certificate is issued and signed by a higher-level CA. When a CA creates a subscriber's certificate, this establishes a *chain of trust*. When another party wishes to communicate securely with the subscriber, it validates the subscriber's certificate using the issuing CA's public key, which is embedded in the CA's own certificate. Successful validation provides assurance that the public key contained in the subscriber's certificate is authentic and bound to the stated identity.

In a PKI hierarchy composed of multiple CAs, certificate validation may require several steps, with each certificate being verified against the certificate of the issuing CA, progressing upward through the hierarchy until the root (top-level) CA certificate is reached. If the relying party ultimately trusts the root CA, then trust can be extended to all subordinate CAs and their subscribers.

Thus, when a third party and a subscriber share trust in a common root CA, secure and authenticated communication becomes possible. Figure 11 illustrates an example of a PKI hierarchy incorporating multiple CAs and certificate chains.

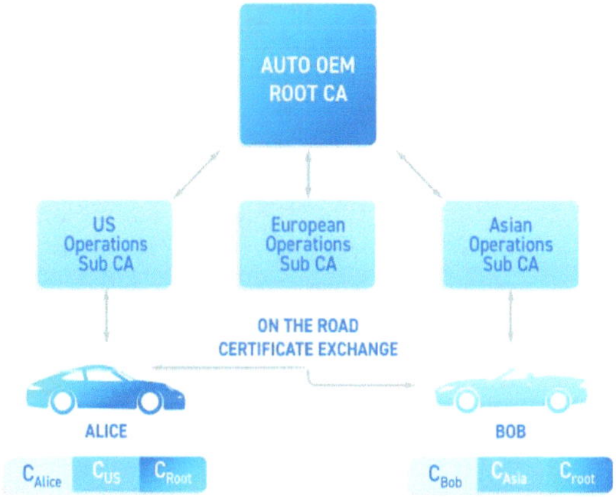

Figure 11: **PKI Hierarchy Example**

Certificate Revocation and Trust in Certificate Authorities

In addition to issuing certificates, CAs can also issue Certificate Revocation Lists (CRLs). A CRL is a list of certificates that are still within their validity periods but which can no longer be trusted due to an issue with the certificate owner (subscriber), such as key compromise or policy violation. Rather than containing public keys, a CRL contains a list of serial numbers corresponding to revoked certificates. Each CRL has its own serial number and validity period and is digitally signed by the issuing CA.

For example, if the private signing key used by a code-signing service were compromised, the issuing CA could add the signing server's certificate serial number to a CRL and distribute the signed revocation list to all subscribers. Any device receiving a software update signed with the revoked key would then be able to detect the revocation and correctly reject the update.

Because CRLs are not always issued or distributed in real time, an attacker may have a window of opportunity to exploit a compromised key before relying parties become aware of the revocation. To reduce this exposure, some systems, typically enterprise systems with online connectivity, query the PKI directly to determine the current status of a certificate before using it. The Online Certificate Status Protocol (OCSP), specified in IETF RFC 6960, is an example of such a mechanism.

To trust a CA, relying parties must have confidence that:

- The CA is managed and operated in a secure manner;
- Its procedures for verifying subscriber identities are reliable; and
- All aspects of its operations are handled with rigor and care.

The primary responsibility of a CA is the protection of its private keys. To achieve this, CAs employ secure hardware such as FIPS 140-2 Level 3–certified Hardware Security Modules (HSMs), along with strict operational controls governing access to cryptographic material. The most security-sensitive root keys are often kept offline, stored in secure vaults, and never connected to a network. Access to these keys is typically governed by carefully scripted, witnessed key ceremonies involving multiple trusted individuals and comprehensive auditing.

When designing a PKI for embedded devices, public CA services, such as those governed by the CA/Browser Forum and offered by providers like Let's Encrypt, are generally not an optimal choice. The CA/Browser Forum standards are designed for the public Internet and primarily address use cases involving unauthenticated clients connecting to authenticated servers. Embedded systems, by contrast, often require mutual authentication, and devices may alternate between client and server roles. The CA/Browser Forum does not permit certificates to support both client and server authentication, which complicates mutual authentication scenarios.

Additionally, the public trust model, where a single root certificate is shared across many unrelated organizations, is often undesirable for embedded and IoT systems. These environments typically require that only known and explicitly trusted entities be allowed to connect and they may require distinct operational policies and practices, requirements best satisfied by a private PKI. Establishing a private PKI may involve developing and operating your own CAs or using a specialized vendor focused on embedded and IoT deployments. Such solutions can provide optimized certificate formats, seamless integration with manufacturing systems for high-volume provisioning, and certificate renewal and revocation mechanisms tailored to the operational constraints of the product.

Public CAs are subject to formal standards, operational requirements, and independent audits. Every CA, including those comprising a private PKI, must publish a Certificate Policy (CP) that defines the technical, business, and legal requirements governing certificate issuance for specific applications. They must also publish a Certificate Practice Statement (CPS) detailing the procedures used to issue, manage, and revoke certificates in accordance with the CP. These documents, along with CA operations, are specified by IETF and ISO standards.

Independent audit organizations regularly assess CA compliance with these requirements. One widely recognized audit framework is WebTrust. Any organization relying on a public or private CA should carefully review its CP and CPS to ensure suitability for the intended application. A successful WebTrust audit provides evidence that the CA's operations have undergone a thorough, professional, and independent review.

Enrollment

The process by which a subscriber device, such as a vehicle infotainment unit or a smart refrigerator, applies for a public key certificate is called enrollment. For IoT devices, enrollment typically occurs during manufacturing, and the exact procedure depends on the nature of the device. In the most secure cases where public keys are used, the device generates its own public/private key pair and stores the private key securely in protected memory. This prevents third parties, such as malicious tester software, from learning the private key. When the tester poses an acceptable risk, or that risk can be mitigated, another method may be used in which key pairs are generated externally and injected into the devices on the manufacturing line. In both cases, the device's public key is sent as an enrollment request to a Certificate Authority (CA) to obtain a device certificate. If the CA determines the enrollment request is accurate and authentic, it returns a public key certificate that uniquely identifies the device and binds the device's public key to that identity.

Enrollment prepares a device to participate in trusted services, and multiple keys and certificates may be required. Good security practice dictates that keys should be used for only one purpose, so multiple services may necessitate multiple keys. Regardless of the device's requirements, enrollment must be performed under secure conditions, not only to prevent information theft or alteration, but also to prevent rogue devices from being enrolled. The enrollment data is highly sensitive, and all factory equipment that handles it must provide high assurances of security.

Certificate Lifecycle Management

Certificates expire and must be replaced in a secure and reliable manner. Certificate validity periods depend on both the application's cryptographic requirements and the expected cryptanalytic security of the signing algorithm. Some certificates, such as those for code signing, may last for a decade or more, whereas certificates for vehicle-to-vehicle communications may only last a week.

Certificate Lifecycle Management (CLM) covers all aspects of certificate management, from issuance to monitoring, inventory, renewal, replacement, revocation, and decommissioning. As discussed, issuance on factory lines has its own requirements to ensure security and authenticity, including the prevention of unauthorized overproduction. Similarly, certificate issuance to fielded products must be carefully designed to ensure security and authenticity. For all cases and revocation policies and procedures must be developed. Focusing on CLM helps ensure specific requirements are not overlooked. For example, a common failure is to allow certificates to expire before obtaining new replacement certificates. This can take products and services offline, impacting availability and possibly safety.

As such, CLM must be addressed as part of specifying a product's security architecture. Today, enterprise IT often lacks comprehensive CLM; sometimes IT staff only have an incomplete, manually maintained list of certificates, which can lead to outages due to the expiration of unidentified certificates. Over the last several years, commercial products have been introduced to help enterprises with CLM, but due to the unique requirements of IoT/embedded products, CLM is best addressed in the architectural stage; it is very difficult, if not impossible, to add after the product is in production.

For the IoT/embedded environment, CLM needs to be automated due to the vast scale of installed products. Such automated systems can help maintain the security posture of deployments by ensuring timely certificate fulfillment and revocation list distribution. Automation eliminates human error, provides audit trails, and can assist in demonstrating compliance with regulatory requirements.

PKI Design Considerations

When designing your PKI, some overall considerations include the following:

- One CA or multiple (Root & sub-CAs)? For a specialized product requiring only a few certificates, it may be appropriate to have a single root CA issue them directly in a controlled physical environment. For high-volume applications, and those obtaining certificates via an enterprise network or over the internet, it is better to separate the root CA from the issuing sub-CAs. An offline root CA is the most secure implementation as it cannot be reached via a network connection. Sub-CAs can be created to service different subscriber groups, such as by geographic area (as shown in Figure 11) or by product. Sub-CAs can be scaled to meet the performance requirements of very high-volume manufacturing lines (e.g., semiconductor). Using multiple sub-CAs limits the impact of a compromise, as the compromise of one will not compromise all. Registration Authorities (RAs) may “front” a CA. The RA authenticates the device requesting a certificate and may interface directly with equipment on the manufacturing line. The RA creates a certificate request on behalf of the device and forwards it to the CA. The CA returns the certificate to the RA, which then sends it to the device. The RA creates an additional security buffer between the CA and the external world and provides a location to host custom interface hardware and software, simplifying the CA build. Clearly, multiple CAs and RAs increase implementation and operational costs; however, the improved security and performance often offset these costs.

- Certificate format. Should your design use an established format, such as X.509v3 or IEEE 1609.2, or a custom structure? This is driven by interoperability requirements and your product's communications and storage capabilities. For instance, a low data-rate channel may dictate a smaller certificate size for timely operation.

- Certificate revocation. Revocation must not be ignored in the design process, as it is difficult to add later. Devices with limited or no communications present a challenge. For instance, a product deep in a mine may require issuing Certificate Revocation Lists (CRLs) on USB sticks and implementing a manual update process. Supporting USB, however, opens other attack avenues that must be addressed in the product design. The Vehicle-to-Vehicle Communication community has a clever arrangement in which passing vehicles compare CRLs, and the vehicle with the most recent list sends it to the other.

- Your PKI and products should be designed to gracefully handle their own certificate expiration and replacement. Failure here could cause products everywhere to cease operating. There are a variety of techniques to address this requirement. One, the use of electors, was previously discussed. Another method is to have the CA whose certificate is about to expire sign its replacement certificate and distribute it. The receiving entity can validate the signature using the old but still valid public key and then add the new certificate. An additional consideration is managing validity periods to allow new certificates to propagate through fielded products before the old certificates expire. This enables products to continue operating even if some devices are offline for a time and delayed in receiving updates.

- Enrollment process. Since IoT devices are typically manufactured on global third-party lines, you must ensure the enrollment process only allows authorized products to receive certificates. This can prevent unauthorized overproduction or knockoffs of your product. You must also design the products to properly generate public/private key pairs in a potentially hostile manufacturing environment. Another critical design consideration is how these global manufacturing lines will continue to operate if internet connectivity is lost.

- Availability. A PKI must be designed to match the operational needs of the products it supports. A PKI supporting a high-volume manufacturing line cannot go offline. Similarly, some systems may be designed to use public key pairs for 30+ years. These keys must be protected against loss to ensure the product and its ecosystem remain operational for their target lifetime. A common secure backup mechanism for private (or other secret) keys is secret sharing, in which the key is split into n shares such that only a subset (m) of the shares is needed to reconstruct the key. This is known as an m-of-n secret sharing scheme. The advantage of this scheme is that it accommodates real-world issues like the loss of some shares due to human error, storage device failure, etc. Note that each share must be protected against unauthorized access and use; however, this approach has the advantage that an adversary must collect multiple shares to mount a successful attack.

Security Requirement Implementation Decisions

Specifying the Details of the Cybersecurity Concept

At this point, the Security Architecture Specification (SAS) contains the Critical Asset list and the Threat Assessment and Risk Analysis (TARA). The next step is to take the security requirements derived from the TARA and develop the overall Cybersecurity Concept for the product and its ecosystem. The term "Cybersecurity Concept" is taken from SAE J3061 and is defined as “a description of the high-level strategy for obtaining Cybersecurity for the feature.” The goal is to define a detailed security architecture that reduces the highest potential risks identified in the TARA to acceptable levels. What constitutes an acceptable level is determined by your industry, company, and customers.

A Cybersecurity Concept can be approached from two directions. One is to start with the identified risks and build the necessary cybersecurity requirements from the ground up to address those specific risks. The other approach is to begin with a concept of a secure system and evaluate how that mitigates the identified risks. The difficulty with the first approach is that it may focus too narrowly on specific risks and ignore or de-emphasize others that could prove critical in the future, the proverbial danger of not seeing the forest for the trees. Our recommended approach is more systematic: begin with the notion of creating a trusted system and then specify how to protect that trust throughout all phases of the product lifecycle.

We begin by mapping the TARA security attributes to the cryptographic methods, message/protocol features, and implementation requirements needed to realize those attributes:

TARA Security Attribute	Cryptographic Mechanism
Confidentiality	Symmetric cipher, PK encryption
Integrity	Hash, HMAC, Digital Signature
Availability	Implementation
Authenticity	Digital Signature, Certificate
Non-repudiation	Digital Signature, Certificate
Privacy	Symmetric cipher, Certificate
Freshness	Message/Protocol feature
Trust	PKI, Implementation

Table14: **Security Attribute – Cryptographic Mechanism Map**

When comparing this table with the TARA security requirements, we can see that in addition to creating implementation requirements for the product, it also generates requirements for enterprise IT, manufacturing, and ongoing product operations and support. These requirements will also impact the policies and procedures for each major element of the product lifecycle.

Other inputs to the Cybersecurity Concept must include any mandated controls or requirements from the target customer (government or industry) that have not been captured elsewhere in the TARA process. Examples include requirements from the US Food and Drug Administration for healthcare products, EU data privacy regulations, or US Department of Defense regulations. Lastly, the cost-of-goods (COGS) target must be reviewed as the Cybersecurity Concept is developed, in case the projected costs exceed this target due to the security requirements. Should this occur, either the TARA risk mitigations must be re-evaluated or the cost objective changed.

Selecting the Appropriate Cryptosystem & Protocols

The selection of the cryptosystem and cryptographic protocols for your product is one of the most important design decisions, as it affects not only the product but also its manufacturing and operations ecosystems.

Information Lifetime and Cryptosystem Selection

Using the lifetime information from the TARA critical asset list and the cryptosystem information from the cryptography primer, the cryptosystem can be specified which matches the lifetimes of the critical assets protected by it. Generally, when selecting a cryptographic algorithm, we will err toward the stronger option (see Table 13), as this provides a cushion against unexpected cryptanalytic advances. This decision is moderated by the availability of hardware support (algorithm acceleration) for the desired algorithms and strengths. If the secure microprocessor required to support the strongest key sizes or algorithms significantly impacts the product's COGS, you should return to the TARA to see if you can either: (i) use a different CPU and perform more operations in software, (ii) use a smaller key size, or (iii) use a different cryptographic algorithm.

Post-Quantum Cryptosystem (PQC) Planning and Implementation

We are currently at the beginning of the transition to the post-quantum cryptographic algorithms previously discussed. NIST guidance deprecates the use of ECC and RSA after 2030. For defense products, this transition will occur sooner rather than later with the US National Security Agency requiring PQC compliance by 2027 for new national security systems. Consumer products will undoubtedly make the transition later. The EU is also proposing PQC readiness by 2030.

PQC planning is particularly important for IoT devices, as they are targets for nation-state attacks. Long-lived critical assets may be compromised if an adversary records classically encrypted data now and decrypts it later using a quantum computer. Furthermore, it is safe to assume that adversary nation-states with quantum computing capability will plan to attack classic cryptographically protected industrial control systems, financial systems, and other critical infrastructure to cripple an opponent. Therefore, all manufacturers of IoT devices should strongly consider transitioning to PQC algorithms as soon as practical to ensure their products and the assets they handle cannot be readily compromised in the future.

Embedded IoT devices will need secure microprocessors with native PQC support to accelerate public key exchange and digital signature methods (e.g., ML-KEM, ML-DSA). Another implementation challenge is key and signature sizes. Per Table 13, for ECDH at a 256-bit security level, the total key size is a maximum of 1024 bits, whereas for ML-KEM at the same strength, it is approximately 12,500 bits. This increase in data volume will require more communication time between parties and may impact product performance if communications bandwidth is constrained.

The good news is that AES, SHA-2, and SHA-3 are expected to remain robust against the capabilities of a quantum computer. Hardware security modules (see below) and software cryptographic libraries with PQC support are now becoming available.

Other Considerations Governing Cryptographic Choices

The cryptographic algorithms, integrity mechanisms, and key/certificate management methods must fit the product's operational environment. It is ineffective to specify the most secure algorithms if they cannot be implemented to meet your performance criteria (e.g., wake-from-power-on time). Consider two examples illustrating the impact of the operational environment on the selection of security mechanisms:

- A product with no external access will need to receive secure firmware updates in a manner significantly different from an online device.
- Digital signatures can't be used on a microprocessor incapable of implementing public key cryptography.

Product COGS are obviously a critical constraint. COGS will restrict hardware component selection, a $200 product will have significantly different compute resources than a $1,000 mobile phone. These hardware constraints ripple through the SAS and force necessary compromises.

This represents the ultimate challenge in the embedded space: to craft the optimum security architecture that meets the TARA requirements while operating within the constraints imposed by the product's target market.

Device IDs (Certificates)

Building trust in the IoT world typically requires that all authorized communicating parties possess unique, immutable device IDs. These IDs underpin the security and trust of the entire IoT embedded ecosystem, from device communication and software updates to feature and configuration control. Device IDs need to be bound to the product's hardware to make them difficult to alter or use on another platform.

For an embedded product, the Device ID typically leverages the CPU's immutable serial number along with a unique public/private key pair. An enterprise OTA server or a manufacturing provisioning server may use specialized hardware (such as a Hardware Security Module, or HSM) to provide a trusted location for storing a unique key pair and other elements that comprise its Device ID.

In practice, the Device ID is the certificate that binds the CPU's serial number to its public key. This approach allows for the exchange and verification of both by a receiving party. Using certificates requires implementing an appropriate digital signature algorithm and establishing a suitable Public Key Infrastructure (PKI), or alternatively, allowing the use of self-signed certificates (signed by the end entity itself). The certificate format may be custom to your application or dictated by the communication protocol, for instance, TLS can use either X.509 or IEEE 1609.2 certificate formats.

In the case of self-signed certificates, they must be distributed in a highly trusted manner. If an attacker manages to insert their own self-signed certificate into this process, trusted operation is compromised. For this reason, self-signed certificates should only be used when establishing a PKI is not feasible.

Message Structures and Protocols

Both secure message structures and protocols must be carefully specified to provide the TARA-required security assurances. They must protect against both message alteration and the spoofing of either the message content or the sender's identity. Additionally, messages must be protected against replay attacks, which could force a recipient to revert to an undesired state or perform an undesired action.

Replay prevention often relies on the concept of freshness. This can be implemented using a version number or a monotonically increasing counter, where the recipient tracks the last received value. Freshness can also be supported using a random number (a nonce) sent by the receiver to the sender, which is then incorporated into the signed message returned to the receiver.

Sometimes, security must be added to an existing protocol that was developed without security considerations. Key management and digital signatures introduce additional data that must be exchanged between entities. Furthermore, since block ciphers operate on fixed block sizes (e.g., 128 bits for AES), messages shorter than the block length must be padded. Some block cipher modes of operation also produce ciphertext longer than the original plaintext. Consequently, adding cryptographic protections to a protocol with a fixed message size may limit the techniques available to you.

For standardized protocols used by your product, such as TLS or SSH, cryptographic algorithm selection is often dictated by the standard. With protocols like TLS, the main decision points involve selecting algorithms and their strengths. Another critical decision concerns the need for interoperability with older protocol versions or other sets of cipher suites. If your product's use cases do not require support for older, potentially weaker cryptographic algorithms, we recommend explicitly excluding them. Even when using a standard protocol, a naïve implementation can introduce vulnerabilities that might be overlooked in the TARA process.

The bottom line is that secure message and protocol design is challenging. We recommend using standard, well-studied secure protocols whenever possible as they can provide the necessary security when properly configured.

Case Study – The Modern Car

Let's examine how a modern car might use cryptography to secure its functionality. Virtually all modern cars are connected to the internet and may contain upwards of 130 or more electronic control units (ECUs) governing its operation. The vehicle receives firmware updates for some of these ECUs via its internet connection. All ECUs are connected to one or more internal buses within the vehicle, such as a Controller Area Network (CAN) bus.

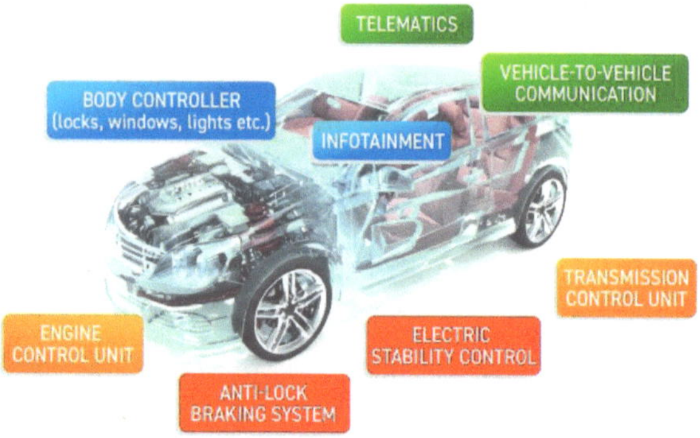

Figure 12: **The Modern Connected Car**

A simple TARA identifies that Over-the-Air (OTA) firmware updates must be protected against compromise and replay, as any unauthorized firmware would compromise the vehicle's operation. In addition, the car must only accept OTA updates from the OEM's OTA system. The OEM also needs to verify the major ECUs are running authorized firmware, as the vehicle's safe operation depends on this. Communications between certain ECUs (such as those for braking, self driving, battery management, and powertrain control) on the vehicle buses must be protected against hackers injecting or replaying commands, again, to ensure safety. Furthermore, ECUs performing safety-critical functions must reject communications from non-safety-critical ECUs. Note that in this context, confidentiality is not a requirement; authenticity is the main concern.

Let's see how we might apply cryptographic techniques and protocols to this scenario. In Figure 12, the Telematics ECU is responsible for communications with the OEM. Each Telematics ECU will generate a public/private key pair and receive a certificate for its public key from the OEM's PKI. This Device ID certificate also contains the ECU's unique ID, which identifies the vehicle in OTA transactions. The OEM's OTA system will also generate a public/private key pair and receive a certificate from the OEM's PKI. With these certificates, both the OEM and the vehicle can authenticate each other and be certain they are communicating with an authorized and authentic endpoint. In this case, mutually authenticated TLS will provide security for the over-the-air communications.

The OTA system will apply a digital signature to the firmware update to protect its integrity and prove its origin. The update package will include a version number (incorporated into the signed data) to prevent the replay of older updates. The OTA system will retain records for each vehicle it updates.

Protecting in-vehicle ECU-to-ECU communications is more challenging due to the use of CAN buses, which have limited bandwidth and defined message sizes. While we cannot allow cryptography to expand the over-the-wire frame size, we can increase the message size (requiring more frames). Because CAN communications support the real-time operation of the car, performance is essential. Therefore, to minimize both message size and the performance impact of cryptography, we'll use symmetric cryptography (AES CMAC) to protect the authenticity of messages on the CAN bus.

To prevent non-safety ECUs from communicating with safety-critical ECUs, we can place them on different CAN buses and use different keys for each group, ensuring they are cryptographically isolated (one bus group cannot decrypt messages from another). Each vehicle's ECU keying must also be distinct from other vehicles so that a compromise of one does not compromise all. The requirements for high performance operation and symmetric key storage require the ECUs to be implemented using microprocessors capable of accelerating the encryption algorithm and securely storing keys so they cannot be easily recovered, even by a service tool.

We also face the practical problem that ECUs can fail and need replacement. When this occurs, we may need to re-key all ECUs using that key group. Alternatively, we could design a key management system that allows the OEM to recreate the vehicle keys and inject only the necessary keys into the replacement ECU, saving service time. Of course, if those keys are distributed from the OEM to a service center, they must be protected in transit and only injected once into an authentic target replacement ECU.

Random Number Generator Implementation

"Anyone who considers arithmetical methods of producing random digits is, of course, in a state of sin." – John von Neumann

As previously discussed, random numbers are essential for key generation and related public key management protocols. If there is any recurrent bias in the random number generator (RNG) output, the keys will be weakened. Taking a 256-bit AES key as an example, we want each bit to be independent and equally likely to be a "0" or a "1." If some bit positions are known to be stuck at "0" or "1," the effective strength of the key is reduced. Another way to view this is that we want the entropy of the RNG, the measure of disorder or variability, to be at least as high as the cryptographic strength we require.

From a theoretical perspective, the best way to obtain sufficient entropy is to sample a quantum process, which ensures each output bit is independent, equally likely, and, most importantly, unpredictable. Examples of quantum noise sources include cosmic background radiation, the avalanche breakdown in a reverse-biased

Zener diode, and resistor thermal noise. Non-quantum sources can also be used. For instance, in digital semiconductor circuits, two popular methods for random data generation are metastable latch breakdown and multiple free-running ring oscillators.

From a practical standpoint, we need our entropy source to operate reliably despite component batch variances, supply voltage variation, general system noise, and temperature fluctuations. We also want to limit an attacker's ability to influence the RNG's operation. Additionally, the random data output of the noise source should be several times higher than the rate at which we draw from it. As a trivial example, if we need 256 bits for a key every second, but our noise source only outputs 256 bits per minute, many keys would be identical - a major flaw.

While the authors built RNGs using quantum noise in the 1980s, these were largely handcrafted and expensive, making them impractical for today's high-volume, low-cost IoT market. To overcome these implementation issues, engineers turned to pseudorandom generators (PRNGs) or Deterministic Random Bit Generators (DRBGs), which use "unpredictable inputs" (seed data) and an algorithm to produce pseudorandom output. The algorithm is chosen to remove statistical bias from the output. The seed data can be externally injected at the time of manufacture or derived from various sources within a product, including a digital or analog true RNG (TRNG). Note that with a DRBG, the same input produces the same output, so the entropic quality of the input seed data is critical for cryptographic use.

Early naïve implementations of RNGs simply used the C library's rand() function. As Dr. von Neumann observed, these developers were "in a state of sin," as this method lacked sufficient entropy and its output was easily determined. The first version of SSL (v1, released in 1995), the precursor to TLS, attempted to improve matters by using the time of day, process ID, and parent-process ID as inputs to its PRNG. However, the resulting entropy was only about 30 bits and easily guessable; an SSLv1 session could be broken in about 10 minutes in 1995. Unfortunately, many IoT product engineers still do not fully understand the intricacies of PRNG design.

The following chart illustrates two IoT devices (green ovals) communicating using TLS with a Google server (blue oval) over a four-hour period in 2021. The red ovals indicate that 80% of the connections repeated random numbers!

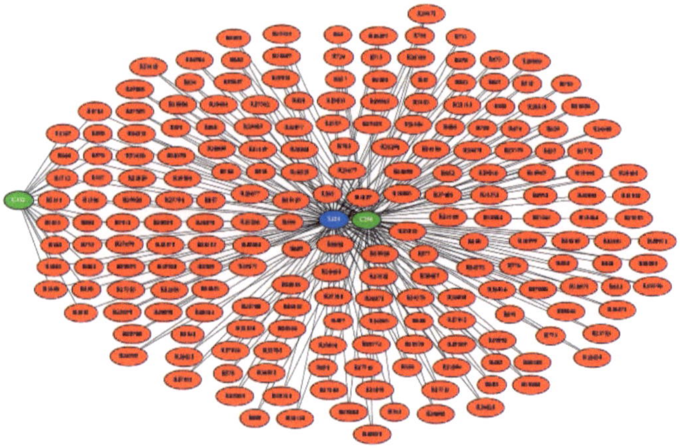

Figure 13: ***Repeating Random Numbers (see Hughes/Diffie paper)***

To help the industry improve, NIST published a series of Special Publications governing RNG design: SP 800-90A, B, and C. These documents cover both Nondeterministic Random Number Generators (NRBGs) and Deterministic Random Bit Generators (DRBGs). Your engineers should study them carefully to better understand the requirements for building and testing an RNG for cryptographic use.

The DRBG approach is the simplest and lowest cost. Properly seeding the generator, however, requires the most effort. If an initial random seed is provided, it must be provisioned securely to prevent interception on the manufacturing line. Furthermore, the seed must be unique per device to avoid all devices generating identical pseudorandom outputs.

Another variation is a hybrid construct, in which the DRBG is initially seeded with a high-quality seed and then periodically updated with local entropy collected from its environment. In this case, the DRBG can function as an "entropy collector."

Implementing either a DRBG or a hybrid version involves additional real-world considerations to ensure proper and secure operation:

- For the hybrid version, after power-on, how quickly will the seed inputs accumulate sufficient entropy to be usable? If it takes a few seconds to gather entropy, the DRBG should block output until it is ready.
- When only low-rate entropy inputs are available (slow entropy collection), and gathering sufficient entropy could take considerable time, designers may choose to store the DRBG state between power cycles for faster resumption. Such states must be highly protected secrets within the system to prevent an attacker from recovering them, as this will likely compromise the RNG and your product. Tamper protection should be considered in this case.
- How well do you know your open-source components? Is the RNG code correct? Nation-states have attempted to alter open-source software in the past, so your development team must actively monitor for such risks.
- Lastly, is the DRBG (or RNG) design you are using certified? If it is implemented in a secure microprocessor, has the vendor validated the design? The FIPS 140 certification program provides confidence that the DRBG is operating correctly. You may have to settle for a design "intended to meet FIPS 140"

standards. A European analog to the NIST document is the German BSI's AIS-20 and AIS-31 standards.

Product Implementation Goals

Locking the Barn Door <u>Before</u> the Horse Escapes...

The goal of the SAS process is to enable you to proactively secure your embedded product, avoiding the need to scramble for fixes post-compromise. Returning to our earlier analogy, we want the hardest, thickest shell protecting the tiniest, soft, tasty core of sensitive critical assets. This is where embedded cybersecurity differs significantly from enterprise cybersecurity, it is possible to lock down an embedded/IoT product comprehensively.

The SAS is about building trust into your product and its supporting ecosystem (e.g., manufacturing services, OTA update services, etc.). The product and ecosystem will remain trusted if every element is identified, all software is authentic, communications are trusted, and the supporting services are implemented and operated in a controlled and reliable manner.

Top-level secure product implementation goals should include the following:

- Secure Boot. Your product wakes from a power-on state, verifies its firmware and environment, and, having determined it is in a known good state, enters operation. This is a crucial defense against malware. From a cryptographic security perspective, such boot tests will verify that the cryptographic accelerator is operating correctly, the CPU is functioning properly, and the RNG is correctly seeded and ready. As part of this process, the CPU will verify that its boot code is authentic and that any subsequently loaded firmware is authentic. This can prevent malware from gaining a persistent foothold in the product. The performance time of secure boot is often an important consideration. Think about getting into your car and how quickly (in human terms) it is running after you turn the key or press the start button. Secure boot must be performed within the operational requirements of the system. It typically involves verifying a digital signature, though optimizations may use a securely computed and stored hash value of the firmware, among other methods. If secure boot fails, the CPU must enter a defined safe state.

- System Module Verification. The CPU implementing secure boot can also verify the authenticity of firmware running in other modules within the total system. For example, returning to the hypothetical vehicle from our earlier case study, the secure-boot-equipped Telematics ECU could verify the firmware running on other ECUs that are incapable of secure boot, confirming they have authentic firmware. Such a step can prevent rogue firmware installed on another system module from running undetected. A strong security objective for systems operating in critical environments is the ability to attest to the proper state of all individual elements/modules, providing confidence that the overall system (e.g., a chemical plant control system and its sensors) is operating from a known good base.

- Secure Cryptographic Implementations and Key Storage. This means that cryptographic algorithms (symmetric ciphers, hash functions, public key algorithms) and the RNG are free from unauthorized interference, typically achieved through hardware implementation. Keys must be securely stored and used so they are unavailable to an adversary. Note that ephemeral "session" keys, used only for a short period, can be created and stored in secure RAM. However, long-term persistent keys (which may be retained for 30+ years) must be stored in non-volatile memory resistant to hardware attacks. Another method for protecting persistent keys is to encrypt them (with integrity protection) and store them in other memory that can be backed up. Of course, the key(s) used to encrypt other keys must themselves be stored in secure memory and protected from loss. Secure protocols should leverage secure hardware to prevent manipulation by an adversary.

- Securely Managed and Operated. Users must be strongly authenticated, with role-based authorization strictly enforced. Strong passwords or, preferably, multi-factor authentication should be required. There must be no default passwords or permanently embedded common secret keys in the product. Commands and configuration data sent to or from the product must be protected against undetected manipulation and should be verifiably authentic. Depending on the context, these commands may also need to be encrypted for confidentiality. Although a secure protocol like TLS may be used, it can be desirable to directly sign command data before transmission. All such data must also be protected against replay.

- Firmware Updates. It is important to understand that a trusted system is not necessarily bug-free. It only means the system is performing as designed and tested. Bugs may still exist, and security vulnerabilities may need patching. Therefore, the system must support software updates over time to maintain security.

- Firmware update packages must be authenticated and integrity-protected; they may also require encryption for confidentiality. Specifically, the product must reject any unauthorized or corrupted updates. Rather than relying on a simple error detection algorithm like a CRC, a strong cryptographic integrity check, such as an HMAC or digital signature, should be used to make undetected alterations impossible. Updates must also incorporate freshness mechanisms to prevent rollback to a prior, insecure firmware version. Data critical to reliable operation, such as calibration data or enabled features, should be similarly protected.

- To ensure system availability, careful consideration must be given to how the product behaves if a firmware update fails. The most robust approach is to use dual memory banks (A/B memory). The CPU operates from one bank while the new firmware is loaded and verified in the second. If verification passes, the CPU reboots using the updated bank. This adds to COGS but ensures availability, making it the preferred approach for safety-critical products.

- Secure Maintenance. Servicing a secure product introduces varying levels of complexity. At the system level, when a product is returned for service, secret keys and other sensitive information must be either erased or protected from recovery by technicians. Service requests should also require authentication. For example, JTAG is widely used to access internal registers and functions in integrated circuits. If left unprotected, JTAG could allow an attacker to extract secret keys from on-chip memory. JTAG locking mechanisms should be designed sophisticatedly, avoiding a single secret key for all chips. Similarly, when a car is serviced, both the technician and the target vehicle should be authenticated so that only specific ECUs on that vehicle are unlocked. The system should also relock itself automatically if the technician forgets to do so.

Hardware Considerations

Product implementation goals ultimately focus on the secure and reliable operation of the product and its support ecosystem. At the heart of these goals is the concept of a Trust Anchor, traditionally defined as an immutable identity. Here, we expand this definition to also include secure compute capability for security functions and secure storage for sensitive data. This enhanced definition creates a functional Trust Anchor that can perform security functions in a trusted manner, giving the product a unique identity and a reliable, trustworthy core. Trust anchors are essential not only to the product but also to the secure support systems in its ecosystem.

A trust anchor must be implemented in hardware to ensure unchanging, reliable operation. In the embedded world, this is typically a secure microprocessor. In enterprise settings, a trust anchor can be implemented using a Hardware Security Module (HSM) or a Trusted Platform Module (TPM), although security-enabled CPUs are also providing this capability, albeit with some concerns regarding their resistance to attack. Let's review these devices in more detail.

Secure Microprocessor

At its simplest, a secure microprocessor is a self-contained single chip capable of providing all the processing power required for the end product. More complex versions are implemented as a System-on-Chip (SoC) that includes application CPUs alongside a secure microprocessor. Many suppliers offer off-the-shelf secure microprocessors, including Infineon, NXP, Renesas, and STMicroelectronics.

A secure microprocessor typically provides some or all of the following capabilities (note that secure boot is essential):

- Immutable ID. A secure microprocessor will have a unique, immutable serial number that can be used for identification.

For example, this ID can be included in commands to ensure they are intended for a specific device and cannot be copied to another product of the same type.

- Secure Boot. Unless its boot code can be verified, the device will not boot, or, preferably, will enter a defined safe state. Secure boot must align with system requirements, which may involve different software loads and occur in stages. The initial boot code is typically stored in mask ROM, making it immutable. This code may validate a bootloader, which then validates the firmware. These steps may use public key digital signatures, MACs, or hash verification. Digital signature verification, while often the slowest, offers the greatest flexibility. The public verification key is usually stored in one-time programmable (OTP) memory, which cannot be erased once written.

  A MAC-based approach requires a secret key stored in secure memory. Unless the CPU generates this key and creates the verification MAC during a special programming step, a unique key and MAC must be generated and loaded into each device on the manufacturing line. Future updates would then require the OTA Update Server to use that device's specific key to compute a new MAC for the firmware package. Using a global key is undesirable, as its compromise would affect all products.

  In the simplest approach, during special phase of programming, the secure microprocessor computes a hash of its firmware and stores it in secure memory. Updates are only possible if the device can be securely placed into the programming phase, with assurance that authorized personnel in a secure location are performing the upgrade.

- When one CPU serves as the verification engine for others on the same chip, ideally the other CPUs should be prevented from running until their software has been verified. Note that the examples discussed here are not the only ways to implement secure boot.

- Random Number Generation. The RNG design uses a FIPS 140/BSI AIS20/31 "approved" or "designed to meet" design. Some secure microprocessors require a seed value to be injected during manufacture. This seed must be either securely created on the manufacturing line and injected, or securely generated centrally and conveyed to the manufacturing line for secure injection. The seed must be unique per device and must not be retained once injected. A secure microprocessor may facilitate the secure storage of DRBG state to maintain entropy between power cycles.

- Hardware Cryptographic Acceleration. Most secure microprocessors accelerate AES and SHA algorithms. Others provide MAC computation, with some supporting a single MAC algorithm and others supporting many. Some can perform key derivation, generating a new symmetric key from a "master" symmetric key. The most advanced secure microprocessors accelerate the computationally intensive public key operations used for key management and digital signatures, while others can implement the actual public key exchange protocol or digital signature sign/verify functions. Hardware acceleration is crucial for fast secure boot times. Ideally, secure microprocessors will have their algorithm implementations validated against NIST test criteria through the Cryptographic Algorithm Validation Program.

- Key Generation. Internal generation of keys in a secure environment is critical for a Trust Anchor.

- Secure Storage. Sensitive data should be stored securely on-chip. Examples include symmetric keys, private keys, DRBG state, and enabled product features. When active tamper detection is used, on-chip memory should be battery-backed so it can be erased upon loss of power, particularly if tampering is detected when mains power is absent.

- Secure Protocol Acceleration. The most expensive secure microprocessors, typically system-on-chips (SoCs), can implement full protocols such as IPsec and TLS on-chip. This may be required for high performance, high security, or both.
- Monotonic Counters. Many cryptographic functions use counters for message freshness or as required inputs for key derivation. Monotonic counters are useful because they only advance, preventing reuse.
- Anti-tamper Features. Some secure microprocessors incorporate features to complicate attacks through external probing or by decapping the chip and probing the die internally. Other security sensors may also be implemented to detect clock glitching, extreme temperatures, or light/radiation. Triggering these sensors results in the erasure of secret data.

The European EVITA project (2011) specified a family of Hardware Security Modules (HSMs) designed for integration into System-on-Chip (SoC) ICs and targeted at automotive applications. This design used a 128-bit security level and predates the standardization of post-quantum cryptography (PQC) algorithms. The EVITA design described three levels of HSMs, distinguished by the level of hardware acceleration they provide. The lowest-level module provides hardware acceleration for AES, a DRBG (seeded by a TRNG), an internal clock, and a monotonic counter. The second level builds on the first by adding public key support in firmware. The highest-level module adds hardware acceleration for public key cryptography operations.

A German consortium of automobile manufacturers refined the EVITA HSM definition and created the Secure Hardware Extension (SHE) design. SHE is equivalent to the medium-level EVITA HSM and is widely used in automotive applications today. It was designed to offer the best trade-off between security, cost, and performance for automotive use. SHE includes secure key storage for 10+ AES keys (implementation-specific) and hardware acceleration for the AES cryptographic function. It does not provide any public key algorithm acceleration. SHE uses the AES-CBC-MAC function to allow the AES accelerator to provide both encryption and hashing.

Adjunct Secure Processors

For systems using standard CPUs without integrated security features, an adjunct secure processor chip can augment the main host CPU. Examples include the Trusted Platform Module (TPM) integrated circuit used in many enterprise PC and server platforms, and the Hardware Security Module (HSM), which is typically a plug-in card for an enterprise server. Some adjunct processors can also be built into the same System-on-Chip (SoC) as the main application processors.

TPM

The Trusted Platform Module (TPM) provides a variant of secure boot known as attested boot. The TPM and the main platform CPU work together to attest to the integrity of the CPU's firmware. This is accomplished by the main CPU generating a hash of each firmware element in its boot sequence before executing it and sending this hash (a "measurement") to the TPM. The TPM then computes and stores a composite value in a specific Platform Configuration Register (PCR). Different PCRs can be used for different firmware components. Note that during this process, the CPU continues booting as measurements are made. This differs significantly from the secure microprocessor's secure boot function, which would cause the system to enter a defined safe state upon verification failure.

To prevent a product from operating with malware, the TPM protects critical data and keys, releasing them only if the PCRs contain the correct values. This is achieved by encrypting sensitive data within the TPM and releasing it to the main system only after PCR validation. In the event of an integrity failure, the PCR values will not match, and the TPM will refuse to release the protected keys and data to the main CPU or peripherals. Full disk encryption often leverages this functionality. The PCR values can also be digitally signed and sent to a remote station to confirm the local system's proper configuration. If a problem is detected, the remote station can restrict the local station's network access, helping to limit the spread of certain attacks. While TPMs are not as flexible as a secure microprocessor, they are inexpensive and enable boot process verification for CPUs lacking native secure boot capability.

Hardware Security Module (HSM)

A Hardware Security Module (HSM) is an intelligent hardware module designed to plug into a standard computer bus. It can store keys and perform a wide variety of cryptographic algorithms, functions, and protocols within a tamper-protected housing. The most widely used standard for evaluating HSM design and implementation is FIPS 140.

HSMs do not provide secure boot for their hosts, but their firmware cannot be altered by an attacker due to a combination of local security controls and required physical access. Because they are standalone, tamper-protected devices, they are suitable for high-trust applications such as Certificate Authorities (CAs), OTA update systems, and manufacturing line security appliances. Note that the host platform's OS and software must also be protected to prevent misuse of the application itself.

HSMs vary in capabilities but share several common requirements:

- High-quality random number generator capable of supporting high output rates.
- Cryptographic algorithm acceleration for supported algorithms.
- Secure storage for secret keys, with the key erasure upon tamper detection.
- Read-only key storage. Public keys aren't secret and do not require the same level of protection as secret keys; however, they must be protected against unauthorized modification or replacement. A common use case is the public verification key used for secure boot image verification. These keys are typically stored in fused, write-once memory, burned in at the factory and never changed afterward. Public keys may or may not be stored within the HSM itself.
- Internal processor to control the HSM and execute cryptographic operations. This processor handles local key management, controls HSM hardware, executes cryptographic algorithms not implemented in accelerator hardware, and manages external communications. HSMs do not allow direct memory access to key memory; instead, the internal processor accepts external requests and provides responses.
- Anti-tamper protection. FIPS 140 specifies different levels of tamper protection. Most HSMs implement Level 2 or Level 3, while very security-critical or defense applications may require Level 4. Additional discussion on this topic follows below.

- Complete protocol acceleration. Some HSMs are expressly designed to accelerate complex protocols such as TLS and IPsec.
- PKCS #11 API to enable programmers to leverage the HSM's functionality from their applications.
- Secure execution environment. Some HSMs allow hosting custom applications on the internal CPU, enabling the creation of secure, tailored solutions.

Anti-Tamper Requirements

Anti-tamper protection is an important design consideration for both a secure IoT device and its support infrastructure which handle various cryptographic keys and other sensitive data. These protections must account for the adversary's capabilities while balancing the product's cost-of-goods. Examples where anti-tamper solutions are required include:

- A system storing a long-term secret in encrypted form, where an attacker could use a debugger to read memory when the secret is available in plaintext.
- Equipment used to protect your gold firmware image or perform key injection on a manufacturer's assembly line.
- Products sold to governments with specific mandated anti-tamper mechanisms.
- Products handling sensitive data (e.g., PLC control logic) deployed in a "hostile," unattended environment accessible to unknown individuals.

Anti-Tamper Goals and Implementation

What are your anti-tamper goals? Is the objective simply to deter a casual attacker, or must it withstand a more determined, sophisticated attack? The TARA will provide guidance for this decision. An overarching goal of anti-tamper design is to delay the attacker's effort to recover a secret, analogous to UL burglary ratings for safes.

A simple IoT product may store all secrets within its secure microprocessor and perform all calculations in internal memory. However, if external memory is required for sensitive data or cryptographic operations, or if direct probing of the CPU is a concern, additional measures must be taken to protect these chips and data buses from probing. Printed circuit boards (PCBs) can be designed to complicate attacks. For instance, in multi-layer PCBs, sensitive data buses should be routed via internal layers, and test points can be eliminated on production boards.

Other physical defenses include securing the housing to prevent unauthorized access, using methods such as adhesive, ultrasonic welding, pressure press fits, or key locks, or simply enclosing the product in a locked rack with limited access. When designing the product enclosure, if vents or holes are present, they should be baffled so that any probe inserted from the outside must make at least one 90-degree turn before making electrical contact with the PCB or components.

Leaving physical evidence of an attack is a common anti-tamper design goal. Decapping a chip is an obvious example. For larger housings, tamper-evident seals, holographic decals, or permanently sealed enclosures (e.g., glued or welded shut) can indicate penetration. Some highly sensitive systems, such as root Certificate Authorities, store critical components in physical safes requiring multiple parties to open when not in use. The root CA cannot be activated until the safes are opened and the system made operational.

More advanced anti-tamper techniques include conformally coating PCBs with a specialized, difficult-to-remove varnish-like coating. Sensitive components can also be covered with tamper shields to prevent direct probing. The most sophisticated shields detect removal, drilling, or cutting from any angle, triggering the erasure of stored secret data upon detection. Opening the physical housing for maintenance purposes may also activate tamper-detection circuits to erase sensitive information. Some devices are designed to erase data if certain environmental thresholds, such as over/under temperature, voltage, or system clock frequency, are exceeded. Others can detect physical shock or changes in orientation and erase data if predefined criteria are met.

Anti-tamper methods also apply at the chip level. Mask layers can be placed under a top metal layer to hinder probing. Alternatively, the die can be conformally coated to make removal without destruction nearly impossible. Some chips incorporate sensors to detect excessive environmental factors or the presence of light where there should be none.

A quick note on data erasure: some types of memory retain a residue of previously stored data even after being "erased" to all zeros. This is why hard disk erasure programs typically overwrite data multiple times with random patterns. Semiconductor memory locations holding sensitive data should similarly be overwritten with random data to prevent extraction of residual state. If keys are encrypted and stored outside the secure microprocessor or HSM boundary, they can be effectively protected by erasing the encryption key itself, often the fastest way to secure a product during a physical attack.

The strictest anti-tamper measures require that detection and erasure circuits remain active even when main power is absent. This necessitates battery backup, which then becomes a maintenance consideration. Once a tamper-detection circuit has been triggered, the product must not be restorable to normal operation by the user.

As previously noted, FIPS 140 provides detailed information on product anti-tamper requirements and evaluation criteria.

Attacks on Cryptosystem Implementations

Although you may have selected a high strength cryptosystem for your product, attacks against its implementation may still pose a risk. For instance, early smart cards were vulnerable to differential power analysis, a technique that examines a chip's power consumption during cryptographic operations, such as an RSA calculation, and uses statistical methods to extract the private key. This style of attack can also target AES and other public-key algorithms. Another method, timing attacks, analyzes the time taken to perform cryptographic operations. Depending on implementation specifics, certain computations may return results sooner or later based on the inputs, potentially revealing private keys. Some early versions of SSL/TLS were susceptible to this type of attack. Countermeasures include altering internal data and circuit design to smooth power consumption from sensitive operations and restructuring algorithms to ensure all execution paths take constant time.

These are examples of side-channel attacks, where an attacker analyzes incidental information emitted by a system, such as power consumption, timing, electromagnetic radiation, or even sound, to infer secrets. It is analogous to a thief observing a home's water meter or lighting patterns to determine occupancy without ever entering. Many variants of side-channel attacks exist, targeting everything from traditional CPUs (e.g., Intel SGX) to virtualized servers in data centers. While a detailed discussion is beyond the scope of this book, such attacks represent an additional risk that must be considered in your Security Architecture Specification (SAS). We anticipate that AI will both refine existing side-channel techniques and uncover new ones in the future. Some chip and HSM vendors may provide assurances regarding their products' resistance to these attacks.

Because these attacks are highly implementation-specific, if your development team lacks expertise in this area, we strongly recommend engaging a cryptography consultant to assist with the analysis.

Software Development (Dev/Ops)

Developing software for a cyber-secure embedded product involves two related sets of requirements. First, the software development process itself must be security-focused. To that end, NIST has published SP 800-218, the Secure Software Development Framework (SSDF), which establishes a set of high-level practices for integrating security into the software development lifecycle. The goal is to reduce the number of vulnerabilities in released software and mitigate the potential impact of the exploitation of any undetected or unaddressed vulnerabilities.

The second set of requirements pertains to the implementation of cryptographic algorithms, protocols, and message structures. As we have seen, side-channel attacks can compromise sensitive data. Developers implementing cryptographic algorithms in firmware must take care to guard against timing attacks and other side channels. Cryptographic implementations should be verified against test suites from the NIST Cryptographic Algorithm Validation Program (CAVP) to confirm correctness.

Cryptographic data must also be handled carefully. Intermediate calculation results and registers used during public-key computations and key derivations must be securely erased once completed. All memory locations used for storing secret keys (whether AES or public-key) must be tracked and securely overwritten when keys are no longer needed or are moved. Note that compilers may sometimes optimize out these erasure instructions if they appear unnecessary. Additionally, non-cryptographic random number generators must never be used for cryptographic purposes, including generating nonces for protocol freshness.

Should your team consider moving away from C/C++ to a memory-safe programming language? Memory-safe languages prevent errors arising from memory mismanagement, such as out-of-bounds access, garbage accumulation, and ownership violations. Examples include Rust, Java, and Python. In 2019, Microsoft reported that over 70% of the Common Vulnerabilities and Exposures (CVEs) they assigned were related to memory safety issues.

Many companies are now using AI to assist in code generation. However, current AI tools are not yet known for producing secure code and likely lack awareness of cryptographic secure-coding requirements. While AI capabilities in this area will undoubtedly improve, human oversight and expert review remain essential.

Of course, general cybersecurity hygiene must still be followed and enforced. Default static passwords and default secret keys shall not be hardcoded into the system. A default password must be forced to change upon first login before the product can become operational. It continues to amaze us how many products shipped today violate this most basic requirement. The same applies to OS hardening. The product's OS should be configured to support only required services, libraries, drivers, and ports. As previously discussed, all cryptographic protocols (e.g., TLS, SSH, IPsec) should be hardened to limit the use of older versions and weaker cipher suites when backward compatibility is not required. Don't forget to lock debugger access when the product transitions from development to production, in order to prevent the recovery of secret or sensitive information.

Before the product is released to manufacturing, its overall security posture should be carefully examined. Software must be thoroughly tested. Static code analysis examines source code without executing it to detect bugs, security vulnerabilities, and deviations from coding best practices. To examine the software while it is running, dynamic code analysis can be performed. This is particularly useful for finding unexpected runtime behaviors. One important tool in the dynamic analysis toolbox is fuzzing. Fuzzing is a technique of feeding external interfaces and protocols (e.g., Wi-Fi, TCP/IP, and TLS) random, invalid, or unexpected inputs to uncover buffer overflows, memory corruption, and other flaws. The classic dynamic test is penetration testing, in which external attackers attempt to gain access to the product. While penetration (pen) testing is valuable, its effectiveness is directly linked to human creativity, resources, and time. Thus, the most effective penetration tests involve large teams of attackers who can study the product, write custom exploits, and repeat attacks over an extended period, which tends to be expensive.

If your team uses AI for code development, static code analysis, dynamic code analysis, and fuzz testing should be considered essential. While the testing methodologies described here will not catch every flaw, it will significantly improve your confidence that all protocols, such as Bluetooth, Wi-Fi, TCP/IP, SSH, IPsec, and TLS, are implemented and configured properly.

Another element that requires oversight and control is third-party software incorporated into your products. Your software team may use open-source code, and some implementations may pull in other open-source components to create the final product. There have been many well-publicized attacks in which open-source code of unknown provenance was incorporated into products, or hackers inserted malicious code into a company's software with the goal of creating vulnerabilities to exploit in the future. These are known as supply chain attacks, and they are having devastating consequences.

We previously described the SolarWinds supply chain attack and its success in penetrating a multitude of high-value companies and government organizations. Note that this attack abused the trust implicit in digital signatures, because the modified code was signed by the legitimate issuer (SolarWinds), it was accepted by target systems as authentic. SolarWinds unwittingly became a malware distribution company during this attack. This underscores the importance of having confidence in your supplier's software development processes to prevent unauthorized code modification (both in development and production) and in their cybersecurity controls and enforcement.

Another attempt to create a supply chain attack was performed against OpenSSH by unknown attackers, most likely belonging to a nation-state. These attackers used social engineering over two years to insert malware into the common xz compression package so that it could be distributed in planned updates to systemd, the default system and service manager for most Linux distributions. This code would have allowed attackers to defeat sshd authentication and gain remote access to the target system. Fortunately, the malware was poorly implemented and caused a performance issue that led to its discovery before widespread distribution. Had it been successful, this would have been a devastating attack for Linux systems.

Lastly, consider two official repositories of third-party software, the Python Package Index (PyPI), and the Node Package Manager (npm), the default package installer for Node.js. Both were established to help developers find and install software developed by third-party communities. Packages in these repositories have limited provenance guarantees and are often pulled automatically by tools used by your developers or by your automated Continuous Integration/Continuous Delivery (CI/CD) systems. Shai-Hulud is a recent example of malware that targets npm and GitHub environments to compromise developer machines and cloud services, steal credentials, exfiltrate data, and provide persistent remote access. It can propagate itself into other legitimate npm packages via compromised accounts. When a modified npm package is incorporated into your application, the malware executes its payload to steal credentials for the attackers. The attackers behind Shai-Hulud remain unknown. Although PyPI and npm are actively removing malicious packages, compromised packages have been downloaded millions of times. The bottom line is that malicious packages are widespread in these repositories and are very difficult to protect against.

While these attacks have targeted enterprise systems, they demonstrate that nation-states and motivated hackers are exploring attack vectors that could also be leveraged against the embedded space. The U.S. government published Executive Order 14028, which describes the need for a Software Bill of Materials (SBOM) to inventory the software used in products and to understand and attest to their integrity and provenance. As the SolarWinds exploit shows, SBOMs need to be created, maintained, and enforced not only by your company but also by organizations supporting your company. An effective SBOM will contain detailed information about the software, including:

- SBOM Author, Software Producer;
- Component Name, Component Version, Software Identifiers;
- Component Hash;

- License;
- Dependency Relationship (direct, transitive);
- Tool Name;
- Timestamp; and
- Generation Context.

SBOMs are typically large and complex, so to aid interpretation and automation, they should be described using standard machine-readable formats like SPDX or CycloneDX. Hashes of component information are used to detect changes, and these hashes must be protected against unauthorized or automated modification without explicit approval. Ideally, your team will create versioned SBOMs to maintain a complete view of changes over time, particularly for regular monitoring of vulnerabilities and updates. SBOMs enable quick determination of whether a product's software is affected when a new CVE is published. Note that SBOMs are designed to be shared so care must be taken to avoid disclosing proprietary information in shared versions.

Securing SCM Repositories

Given recent attacks on code repositories, it is essential to ensure that your Software Configuration Management (SCM) systems are secure and regularly backed up to allow recovery in the event of a compromise. Many online guides detail how to secure repositories, whether using Git or another SCM system, so we won't elaborate here. Suffice it to say that your engineering team must prioritize this. SCM repository security is critical to preventing theft of your proprietary software or its augmentation with malware.

Integrating Security into Agile Sprints

The Agile methodology is widely used in software development today. However, with its focus on breaking projects into small, sprint-based tasks, overall security requirements can be easily overlooked. To ensure security is consistently addressed throughout firmware development, we recommend the following:

- Treat security requirements as first-class backlog items, using security user stories that include specific security acceptance criteria. Develop dedicated security tasks such as threat modeling, code scanning, hardening, and configuration reviews. This makes security requirements visible and actionable in the backlog.
- For every sprint, define a "security definition of done." This ensures tasks like static code analysis are performed and security acceptance criteria are verified. By explicitly identifying when security work is complete, these tasks cannot be postponed or omitted.
- Integrate security into sprint planning so that security requirements are explicitly addressed for each story. Assign a Security Champion to each team to maintain focus on security throughout the development cycle.
- Track security requirements across releases and perform security validation within the sprint. This prevents security testing from being delayed until the end of the development cycle.
- Include explicit hardening sprints dedicated to security-focused improvements and remediation.
- Maintain a wiki or living security requirements document accessible to all teams. This could include the SAS or relevant extracts, helping ensure a common vision and consistent understanding of security goals.
- Prioritize keeping third-party dependencies up to date. Awareness of newly published CVEs related to your core

dependencies is critical to preventing the release of vulnerable software. Many package managers, such as npm, now report vulnerable package versions during installation and provide guidance on which versions to migrate to.

Secure Product Manufacturing

Producing a reliable product that operates as promised for your customers is a well-understood challenge. Manufacturing a secure product, however, imposes additional requirements to ensure devices are programmed correctly and that cryptographic keys remain secret. These requirements should already be identified in the product's Security Architecture Specification (SAS).

Whether your product is an AI semiconductor chip, a video doorbell, a smart TV, an industrial control platform, or a defense system, it is essential to guarantee that only authorized firmware and configurations are present, and the SAS will mandate this. Given that many IoT products are manufactured on third-party lines, being able to ensure trust and have unforgeable accountability in these environments is critical.

The key lies in recognizing that digital assets are simply another asset type to be managed on the factory floor, albeit with strict security controls. Today, Manufacturing Execution Systems (MES) can track physical assets like displays, tires, microprocessors, and engines from inventory through assembly to the final product. We can apply the same principle in the digital realm by creating a digital asset management infrastructure to manage assets such as gold firmware images, calibration files, digital IDs, cryptographic keys, and product feature controls. Management of these assets encompasses:

- Secure generation of various asset types;

- Controlled ingestion of external assets and their secure storage;
- Secure distribution of digital assets only to the factory lines where they are consumed;
- Metering these assets on the production line; and
- Ensuring availability of the digital assets on manufacturing lines.

Let's examine these capabilities in more detail. The SAS describes the digital assets used by your product, and subsequent engineering documents will fully specify them. The generation of these assets and their secure handling will be controlled by the digital asset management platform on a per-product basis. This generation must be timely and secure, making performance critical. The management platform will need to incorporate one or more HSMs to perform sensitive calculations (including proper key generation) and securely store the results for subsequent distribution. It must also interface with the software release system to accept the signed gold firmware image for injection into products on the manufacturing line.

The gold firmware image must be kept off third-party servers to protect intellectual property, complicate reverse engineering, and prevent its direct use in building cloned products (a digital signature prevents alteration but not copying). While gold firmware images are not specific to individual devices, other device-specific data may need to be handled and injected by the digital asset management system. If your products will be incorporated into another company's system, they may require you to securely manage their assets as well. This could necessitate interfacing your digital asset management platform with a cloud service provider used by the other company to pull specific assets for distribution.

Digital assets must be conveyed securely to the manufacturing lines where they are consumed. This means the digital asset management platform must be aware of your product's manufacturing locations. Assets should be metered out to prevent overproduction and reduce the risk of theft or misuse. If Product A is built in Vietnam and Product B in China, neither site should have assets belonging to the other. Similarly, if multistage asset injection is required, such as installing firmware and a public validation key at Location 1, injecting secure feature data at Location 2, and finally injecting JTAG locking information at Location 3, the platform must accommodate this workflow.

Note that some third-party data also requires protection on manufacturing lines. A classic example is HDCP content protection keys, which are centrally generated by Digital Content Protection LLC and provided to licensees for injection into their chips. Failure to protect against misuse (e.g., multiple injections of the same key) or loss of keys (theft from the contract manufacturer) can trigger liquidated damages of up to US $8 million.

While we can centrally control these assets, we also need secure endpoints on the manufacturing lines to keep sensitive data off the manufacturer's IT network and testers. This requires a digital asset manager secure endpoint, typically using an HSM, which can store assets and meter them out to products on the assembly line at the required rate. Performance demands may range from hundreds of thousands or millions of chips per day to hundreds of more sophisticated devices. This metering function often involves interfacing with a wide variety of testers used by different manufacturers.

Asset availability on global lines must be carefully managed to account for time delays and internet outages. Slowing down a manufacturing line increases costs, and an internet outage that halts production is cost prohibitive. For these reasons, some assets can be generated locally at the endpoints associated with specific manufacturing lines. For the highest security levels, a cryptographic tunnel can be established from the secure endpoint to the secure microprocessor inside your product, ensuring injected assets are never externally available in plaintext.

Because the secure endpoint is trusted, it can provide an unforgeable audit trail of every device programmed, independent of the contract manufacturer's reports. This gives you an accurate digital asset inventory per product and eliminates the manufacturer's ability to overproduce or clone products.

Digital asset management, combined with your product's security architecture, can also ensure that a product is not fully operational until it passes through all manufacturing stages. This helps prevent "product loss" and subsequent grey market availability.

This system, in combination with code signing, can also be used to prevent counterfeit parts dependent upon firmware driver updates. For instance, a large semiconductor firm faced an issue in China where chips from discarded devices were being re-labeled as new and sold with the latest software drivers. Digital asset management was used to address this by verifying the immutable chip ID against internal records. If the chip was authorized, a driver package was assembled and signed exclusively for that specific chip.

Both the central digital asset management platform and the secure endpoints must be hardened against attack. Since these are typically server-based systems, traditional enterprise cybersecurity measures, such as OS hardening, multi-factor authentication (MFA), and role-based access control, should be applied. Both elements should also be tamper-protected due to the sensitive nature of their operations. The secure endpoint is particularly at risk, as it may reside on the open floor of a contract manufacturer's facility in another country.

The secure management and control of digital assets in the manufacturing environment are essential for meeting SAS requirements to protect critical assets. It also enables you to demonstrate to customers that digital assets—including theirs—are handled properly and that products are shipped in a reliable and accurate configuration. As this discussion illustrates, developing a digital asset management platform is non-trivial due to the variety of required interfaces (human, enterprise, and third-party systems), stringent security requirements, and performance demands. Fortunately, digital asset management platforms are available from specialist providers, allowing you to avoid the cost and complexity of building one from scratch.

Additional Secure Product Infrastructure

The SAS feature set will determine the nature of any additional secure product infrastructure required to support the product over its lifecycle. Such supporting infrastructure will likely include a Public Key Infrastructure (PKI), a code signing system, and an over-the-air (OTA) update system. Other services may include a JTAG lock/unlock service or a feature control service.

Public Key Infrastructure (PKI): A PKI may be required to issue certificates to all components of the infrastructure, from the code signing system and digital asset management components to individual products (their digital IDs). This PKI will typically consist of a root CA, possibly one or more intermediate CAs, and leaf CAs at the lowest level. The root CA will likely be common to all products, while lower CAs may be designed to serve different products or geographic regions. In regions where governments require access to signing keys, entirely separate PKIs may be necessary to limit compromise across the entire product line. In cases where each device generates its own key pair and the public key must be securely acquired for inclusion in the device ID certificate, the PKI must interface with the digital asset management platform.

All CA key pairs must be protected against loss, with the root key being the most critical. Typically, this key is split using an *m-of-n* secret sharing scheme, with shares distributed to trusted personnel, physically secured, and all access audited. Key protection is especially vital for embedded products with limited functionality that cannot securely replace a root key themselves. Loss of a root key in such cases could necessitate visiting every deployed product for updates, a prohibitively costly undertaking.

Code Signing Infrastructure: To meet SAS requirements for secure boot, a code signing infrastructure is required to sign firmware. It can also sign product-specific data, such as calibration data, where integrity and provenance are critical. Similar to the PKI, code signing keys may be separated by geography and product. While integration with the software development environment is desirable, strong access controls are essential to prevent unauthorized signing. We recommend requiring at least two-person approval for code signing, which also serves as a checkpoint to confirm all required testing has been completed. To prevent misuse, a separate test code signing infrastructure should be available for development, using different keys to ensure test code and data cannot function in production products. The production code signing infrastructure must incorporate HSMs and be hardened similarly to the digital asset management platform.

Over-the-Air (OTA) Update System: OTA updates require a sophisticated system to perform timely, managed, and secure updates across a potentially vast and complex product ecosystem. At a high level, the OTA system uses digital signatures to sign updates, ensuring recipients can verify authenticity and authorization. It will need one or more certificates from the PKI for its update signing keys, which must be hosted in an HSM. Like the code signing service, the OTA platform must have strong operational controls to prevent the automated distribution of unauthorized software. To minimize data transmission, the OTA service may compress firmware or distribute difference (also known as delta) updates. To protect intellectual property, TLS or other confidentiality-providing protocols can secure tunnels between the OTA system and target devices. The system must manage updates across different geographic regions (which may require different software) and track targets that were not updated for retry attempts. For safety-critical applications, such as automotive systems, the update system may also need to collect driver/owner consent to limit corporate liability. OTA platforms can maintain a detailed history of all updates to fielded products, aiding in issue resolution, ensuring uniformity, and reducing liability.

With this infrastructure, feature control becomes a possible add-on service. Using cryptographic services, feature control enables fine-grained management of a product's capabilities. Examples include sending signed calibration files to a vehicle ECU to adjust engine operation during service, or performing challenge-response functions for JTAG lock/unlock in chips or ECU lock/unlock for service access.

Lifecycle Management for the Secure Product Ecosystem

The digital assets associated with a secure product must be managed throughout its entire lifecycle. While we have discussed asset management in the manufacturing stage, what happens over a product's operational lifetime? Lifecycle management takes the long view, ensuring that the product can be manufactured efficiently and remains secure and functional over its lifespan. Although it focuses primarily on cryptographic keys and certificates, lifecycle management must also monitor and manage other secret information, feature enablement, and software updates for deployed products. Additionally, the software development environment supporting the product must be maintained so that future vulnerabilities can be promptly patched.

The overarching lifecycle requirement is to catalog these assets so they can be effectively managed. Such a catalog will likely include:

- Cryptographic keys
  - Symmetric
  - Asymmetric
- Digital IDs
  - X.509 certificates
  - Custom certificates
  - External service tokens (e.g., OAuth)
- SBOM & Device Status
  - Development packages (proprietary; open source)
  - Product firmware releases (including authorization for production release)
  - Firmware/feature current state by fielded product
    - Update records of targets, firmware/features enabled/other soft assets
    - User permissions collected for each update
- User Identity & Access Management
  - Development
  - Support/repair personnel (in-house / third-party)
  - Customer

Let's examine each of these in more detail.

For cryptographic keys, we are concerned with their sources, lifetimes, and availability. If symmetric keys need to be managed, they are likely sourced from an external provider, for example, for content management schemes. Their consumption on the factory line must be monitored to prevent inventory exhaustion and production line stoppages. Symmetric keys generated by the product itself are not a management concern, as their local generation and usage will have been addressed in the SAS.

Asymmetric (public/private) keys must be tracked and managed according to SAS use cases. For instance, an individual asymmetric key pair used for a unique device identity may last for the life of the product, while the CA(s) and code signing key pairs may need to be periodically changed as described in the SAS. What is extremely critical is that none of the longer-term or permanent keys are lost if there is no "automatic" replacement process available. For example, some vehicles may have a 30-year lifetime and may not be able to change the OEM root CA public key or the OEM code signing public key if they are programmed into one-time programmable memory. If the OEM loses the private signing key associated with either of these embedded public keys, all affected vehicles would need to return to a service site for a new ECU installation, a situation to be avoided at all costs. Lifecycle management for these long-term keys entails developing robust policies, procedures, and practices to ensure they cannot be lost.

Lifecycle Management for Digital IDs and Other Assets

As we've seen, Digital IDs commonly take the form of X.509 certificates or proprietary certificates. These certificates contain the public key of the subject, such as a device or code signing system, and typically expire after a defined period. The management system must ensure they are replaced before expiration to prevent infrastructure services or products from going offline. The SAS will specify the use cases and lifetimes for these key pairs and certificates.

Other forms of Digital IDs used in the IoT space must also be managed. For example, standard programmatic authentication and authorization methods, such as OAuth tokens, JSON Web Tokens (JWTs), and API keys, are prized targets for attackers because they provide access to internal corporate services and data. Token signing keys must be stored and used securely, changed frequently, and revoked when necessary. Given their widespread use, the management of these tokens should be automated to ensure timely control and comprehensive coverage across all applications.

SBOM management is essential for maintaining the security posture of both the development environment and fielded products. While we have already detailed the development-side SBOM, a similar approach is needed to track each fielded device's current configuration, including firmware versions, enabled features, and other relevant data. Interoperability is generally less of a concern on the device side, allowing more flexibility in how this data is represented within your organization. For safety-critical products, it is advisable to collect operator or owner acceptance or denial of any upgrade to aid in liability mitigation.

Just as in the enterprise space, users and their privileges must be managed throughout the product lifecycle. A structured lifecycle process is appropriate here, as employees and customer personnel are not static. On the development side, we recommend programmatically enforcing the decision to promote code to production release. Your lifecycle management platform can require multiple authorized signatures before allowing firmware release, creating an audit trail that documents when software changes were made and who authorized them. This also helps ensure that the released code base contains only authorized and authentic firmware.

User management in the embedded space can be more complex if products are serviced by third parties. This is explored further in the following section on Secure Product Maintenance.

Secure Product Maintenance

A secure product introduces additional requirements for supporting it throughout its lifecycle. For instance, depending on your SAS, the product may need to be unlocked to enable servicing. This could involve unlocking the JTAG port on a chip, re-enabling debugger access on a CPU, or commanding the system to enter a debug state. Clearly, the person or entity requesting the unlock must be authenticated and verified as authorized for this function. Authentication of the service tool itself may also be necessary.

Identifying and authorizing service personnel within your organization is relatively straightforward compared to authenticating third-party personnel. Validating test equipment is more complex and depends on the type of equipment and the attestations it can provide. The device unlock function should either time out, automatically returning the product to its operational locked state, or the service program must ensure the product is restored to a secure state before service completion.

Such systems already exist; for example, the automotive industry uses schemes in which OEMs validate third-party service shops, technicians, and their approved tool sets. These practices offer clear security benefits. However, if your revenue stream includes a service component, they also become business-critical concerns that warrant attention at the C-suite level.

End-of-Life Decommissioning and Anti-Tamper Concerns

End-of-life (EOL) decommissioning requirements for secure products depend on the sensitivity of the information they contain. For an endpoint device, it may be sufficient to place its device ID certificates on a Certificate Revocation List (CRL) or, for short-lived certificates, rely on their imminent expiration, in either case, preventing the product from participating in a network of other products or from receiving other services such as firmware updates.

For highly sensitive systems, such as a CA or code signing system, the HSM and storage media (hard drives or solid-state memory) must be securely wiped and physically destroyed to prevent data recovery. For other systems, like weapons systems that may fall into unfriendly territory, you may need to incorporate anti-tamper logic to erase all critical software and firmware IP and, where feasible, destroy the hardware itself.

Proper EOL decommissioning is essential to maintaining the long-term security posture of the product and its ecosystem.

Additional Cybersecurity Considerations

In the preceding chapters, we have described the requirements for designing, manufacturing, and operating a secure embedded/IoT product throughout its lifecycle. This chapter addresses additional considerations for enhancing enterprise cybersecurity practices to support product security.

Policies and Procedures

Cybersecurity, and cryptography in particular, depends on meticulous attention to detail and proper implementation. These areas require specialized knowledge that should be institutionalized within your company to ensure consistency across projects and teams. The most effective way to achieve this is by creating and maintaining comprehensive policies, procedures, and guidelines that cover the entire secure product lifecycle, from development and manufacturing to operation and end-of-life.

A corporate best practice guideline for secure product design, emphasizing the principle of "secure by design," should include topics such as:

- Cryptosystem selection guidance;
- OS hardening requirements;
- Secure boot implementation;
- Device hardening requirements (JTAG lock, debugger disablement, USB port disablement, test point removal, etc.);
- Secure coding guidance (use of memory-safe languages, secure erasure of intermediate cryptographic computations, resistance to timing attacks, elimination of permanent or default passwords, etc.);
- PCB layout and trace routing practices to hinder physical attacks, including removal of unnecessary test points;
- Protection of sensitive data (e.g., RNG state, cryptographic keys) from physical attacks;
- User authentication and authorization protocols;
- Planning for firmware updates, whether OTA or other methods;
- Planning for key and certificate changes; and
- Testing requirements (cryptographic algorithm/ protocol validation, static/dynamic code analysis, fuzz testing)

Given that cryptography and cybersecurity are constantly evolving, this guide must be regularly reviewed and updated to remain current and relevant.

Alongside institutional documentation, regularly training your software development engineers in secure coding practices will provide long-term benefits to your organization.

Other corporate documentation should be added or updated to address the following:

- Formal Security Architecture Specification (SAS): Its use should be mandated within the product development process, as described in this book.
- Software Release Security Checks: The release process should require security testing (static/dynamic code analysis, fuzz testing). At least two sign-offs, such as from the developer and manager, should be required for any code release to production, ideally enforced programmatically.
- OTA Update Authorization: Launching an OTA update campaign should require multiple authorized signatures to ensure only approved updates are distributed.
- Disaster Recovery/Business Continuity: These plans should be enhanced to explicitly address the protection of long-term keys, such as CA root keys and code signing keys.
- Manufacturing Policies: These should be revised to cover the secure handling of gold firmware images, cryptographic keys, and other sensitive data on both internal and third-party manufacturing lines. Audit requirements to detect unauthorized overproduction should also be considered.

- User Management: Identity and authorization protocols may need to be extended to users of your secure infrastructure, including manufacturing partners, service providers, and customers. Multi-factor authentication (MFA) should be required for all users.

It is unlikely that SBOMs are currently used across your organization. Developing policies and procedures for their creation, use, and maintenance will require dedicated effort. Additionally, your legal team will likely need to update existing contracts and ensure new agreements require suppliers to maintain and provide SBOMs.

Proactive monitoring of Common Vulnerabilities and Exposures (CVEs) is essential for maintaining the security posture of both your product and its ecosystem. Ensure your cybersecurity team has the appropriate tools and staffing to perform this function promptly and effectively.

Consider conducting an annual or bi-annual cybersecurity review of your products and supporting infrastructure. This helps confirm they continue to operate as intended and allows for the timely identification and resolution of any emerging issues.

Enterprise Cybersecurity is Still Required

Although this book focuses on embedded and IoT security, these products inevitably intersect with enterprise IT systems for their implementation, manufacturing, and operation. Consequently, enterprise cybersecurity is a critical component of the product's overall security posture.

Secure embedded/IoT products will expand the range of systems managed by the enterprise IT department. The digital asset management platform, PKI components, code signing system, and

OTA service platform must integrate with your corporate identity and access management system. Unless outsourced to specialized providers, these platforms will require ongoing maintenance by your IT staff, including periodic updates. Interconnections between these platforms and any distributed components should use secure, authenticated protocols such as TLS or IPsec with certificates, which must themselves be carefully managed. Additionally, digital asset management systems deployed on third-party manufacturing lines must connect securely back to the central management platform using these authenticated protocols.

There has been much discussion recently about "secure by design," based on two main principles: (i) your products, when shipped, should not contain vulnerabilities, and (ii) your customers should not need to be cybersecurity experts to properly configure and integrate your products into their IT environment. Your customers should not have to harden your product or perform other security steps requiring deep IT knowledge. In our experience, this principle is especially important in global third-party manufacturing environments, where a fully configured, secure system that can simply be "plugged in" to the manufacturing IT network benefits all parties involved.

Standards & Regulatory Compliance

The number of cybersecurity standards for products continues to grow. Some are generic, such as FIPS 140 (Security Requirements for Cryptographic Modules), while others are industry-specific, like SAE J3061 (Cybersecurity Guidebook for Cyber-Physical Vehicle Systems). Appendix A provides a brief overview of relevant standards. These standards codify best practices and serve as a reference for your developers and product managers. By complying with established standards, rather than developing proprietary approaches, especially for cryptographic algorithms and protocols, you can help mitigate corporate liability in the event of a cybersecurity incident. While cryptographic algorithms are based on computationally complex problems and cannot offer ironclad security guarantees, using NIST or EU-specified algorithms provides a recognized "safe harbor."

For general embedded cybersecurity guidance, we recommend FIPS 140, the NIST SP 800 series, and the EU Common Criteria (ISO/IEC 15408 series). While most of the world accepts the cryptographic algorithms specified in these standards, China and Russia have their own approved algorithms. Note that formal compliance certification by a third-party lab may be required for products sold to governments or specific countries.

Governments worldwide are working to improve the cybersecurity of products in the global marketplace. While many efforts have focused on publishing guidelines, regulatory requirements are increasing as industries are pushed to build more robust products. Examples of current guidelines include:

- U.S. CISA, along with its domestic and global partners, has published important guidelines such as Secure by Design – Principles and Approaches for Secure by Design Software and Secure by Demand: Priority Considerations for Operational Technology Owners and Operators when Selecting Digital Products.
- The U.S. Federal Communications Commission is launching its "Cyber Trust Mark" program, administered by UL Solutions. This voluntary program applies to wireless consumer IoT products, and products meeting its cybersecurity requirements may display the mark.

- The U.S. Food and Drug Administration issued Cybersecurity in Medical Devices: Quality System Considerations and Content of Premarket Submissions, providing guidance to industry and FDA staff on cybersecurity for medical devices. Notably, it emphasizes threat modeling, security architecture, and the use of an SBOM.

- The NIST IR 8259 series and the European ENISA Baseline Security Recommendations for IoT were developed specifically for IoT device cybersecurity. In general, the NIST SP 800 series offers extensive guidance across cryptographic and IT cybersecurity domains.

The regulatory environment is complex, varying by government and industry. As such, we will not attempt to cover it in detail, but we do wish to highlight one significant market-wide regulation from the EU that will soon have broad impact: the European Union's 2024 Cyber Resilience Act (CRA), Regulation 2024/2847, which establishes mandatory cybersecurity requirements for all products with "digital elements." The purpose of the CRA is to improve baseline cybersecurity across the entire digital ecosystem.

A "product with digital elements" is broadly defined as any software or hardware product, or combination of both, that processes digital data and can connect to other digital products. It covers products such as operating systems, browsers, certain IoT devices, industrial digital components, smart home devices, network equipment (routers, switches), and security software (antivirus, VPN, identity management). It also includes digital products marketed for security purposes, such as secure microprocessors and HSMs. Exemptions are available for medical devices, automotive systems already regulated under EU legislation, aviation-certified products, defense/national security products, and marine equipment.

This regulation establishes "secure-by-design" requirements throughout the product lifecycle. Manufacturers must ensure that their products:

- Are designed and developed following recognized cybersecurity practices.
- Are free of known exploitable vulnerabilities at release.
- Implement proper authentication, secure defaults, logging, and protection against manipulation.
- Include secure update mechanisms (with automatic updates required for most consumer products).

Manufacturers must establish coordinated vulnerability disclosure programs and maintain a vulnerability management process for at least five years. Security updates must be provided free of charge to users. An SBOM is required, along with documentation for all components and supply chain dependencies. Manufacturer development processes must follow a secure development lifecycle, and the regulation places explicit requirements on supply chain cybersecurity.

Additionally, manufacturers must report when a vulnerability is actively exploited or when a severe cybersecurity incident affects the product. The initial report is due within 24 hours of detection and must be submitted to ENISA (the EU cybersecurity agency) and the relevant national CSIRT (Computer Security Incident Response Team).

Conformity assessment ranges from self-assessment for less critical products to mandatory EU cybersecurity certification (such as Common Criteria) for "critical" products. Penalties can reach up to €15 million or 2.5% of global annual revenue, whichever is higher. Vulnerability and incident reporting rules begin applying in

September 2026, with full compliance mandatory by December 2027.

For companies selling products in the EU, this regulation deserves close scrutiny to determine whether and how your products are covered.

Cybersecurity as a Revenue Enhancer

Embedded/IoT cybersecurity is not merely a cost driver, it can significantly enhance corporate revenue by introducing new levels of accountability, trust, and flexibility into your products.

The active provisioning of products on third-party manufacturing lines creates an accurate, unforgeable audit trail of production. This eliminates product theft and unauthorized overproduction while preventing losses from counterfeit goods. In the semiconductor industry, for example, it can prevent die that fail parametric testing from being packaged surreptitiously and entering the gray market.

Cryptography can help assure safety by ensuring that only authorized products and components are used together as shown in the following examples:

- An authorized medical sensor can be cryptographically verified before pairing with a medical head-end device, helping ensure patient safety and protecting revenue.
- A replacement battery pack for a vehicle can be authenticated before use, improving safety during operation and charging.
- Replacement modules for an industrial control system can be guaranteed authentic, helping customers maintain their cybersecurity posture while securing your service revenue.

Feature upselling represents a significant revenue stream for cybersecure products. Tesla pioneered this approach by offering to enable enhanced driving capabilities for an additional fee. Similarly, a vehicle OEM could use signed feature commands to support the engine tuner market while limiting powertrain liability, providing cryptographic proof that the owner accepts any reduction in warranty coverage due to the modification. Tamper-proof cryptographic configurations also enable versioning of products on the factory floor without changing the hardware bill of materials, offering new product flexibility and improved manufacturing efficiency.

Markets are increasingly sensitive to cybersecurity. Strong cybersecurity is a powerful product differentiator in the sales cycle. For a manufacturer in need of a control system, a solution that is secure from day one will prevail over an insecure alternative that introduces vulnerabilities from the outset.

The Hard Question – Does Your Team Have the Expertise?

"In theory, there's no difference between theory and practice. In practice, there is." – Benjamin Brewster

As an executive, determining whether your team possesses the necessary embedded cybersecurity lifecycle expertise is a difficult yet crucial question that must be answered honestly. As we have shown, achieving robust cybersecurity requires a skilled, multidisciplinary approach, spanning legal, engineering, manufacturing, and support functions. Moreover, the proper implementation of cryptography demands not only algorithmic implementation knowledge but also specialist knowledge of current attack vectors and defense techniques.

Consider the following examples:

- In this book, we discussed timing attacks against certain cryptographic algorithms. Code that is optimized solely for performance may inadvertently expose the implementation to such attacks, as countermeasures often conflict with speed optimization.

- Years ago, at a cryptography conference, the random number generator (RNG) design for a bank ATM was scrutinized. The engineer had implemented a design from a popular cryptography book but failed to turn the page, where the text explicitly warned against using that design for cryptographic systems. The engineer lacked specialized expertise and the product was sold containing a critical vulnerability.

- In a more recent case, an automotive OEM was building a Certificate Authority (CA) using a required cryptographic algorithm and a proprietary certificate format. Although they used a Hardware Security Module (HSM), it did not natively support the required cryptography within its tamper boundary. An external review show that the implementation was easily breakable because the team had misunderstood the underlying mathematics and misused the HSM.

These examples illustrate that, without proper expertise, products can ship with critical security flaws from day one. In the embedded cybersecurity domain, there is indeed potential for "many a slip 'twixt the cup and the lip."

On the multidisciplinary front, consider the manufacturing IT challenges. Does your team understand the manufacturing environment and the various tester types that must be interfaced with for digital asset injection? Can the provisioning system meet the throughput demands of production lines with different bandwidth constraints, from sneaker net to gigabit? Has the team planned for internet outages lasting hours or even days? If your provisioning platforms are new, will third-party manufacturers accept the risk of using unproven equipment on their lines?

If there is uncertainty in any of these areas, engaging consultants who are expert in security architecture and secure product development and leveraging specialized product offerings from suppliers specializing in digital asset management may be the answer. The security architecture specification phase is so critical to the entire product lifecycle that external expertise can guide and augment your team cost-effectively. Third-party services are also available to assist with product certifications such as FIPS 140, Common Criteria, and WebTrust.

The make-versus-buy decision is always challenging, but given the complexities of implementing strong cybersecurity across the lifecycle, a hybrid approach is often the most effective path forward.

Epilogue – A Life's Work in Trust

The world has been trying to secure the enterprise for decades. How's that going? The IoT/embedded world can, and must, do better.

The enterprise environment is extremely complex, with a vast array of applications, heterogeneous networking environments, and users of widely varying skill levels. The IoT/embedded space, by contrast, is fundamentally different: devices typically support a single application, operate in controlled environments, and serve a very limited number of users. Even mobile phones, which host a multitude of applications, tend to be more secure than general enterprise IT systems due to the strong controls built into both the devices and their supporting ecosystems.

As a C-suite executive, if your development team suggests that traditional enterprise measures, such as a firewall, network segmentation, a VPN, or antivirus software, are sufficient for your product, send them back to the drawing board. Challenge them to design a product with security built in from the ground up. If corporate silos are preventing your world-class product from achieving strong cybersecurity, you must compel those silos to cooperate.

Electric cars did not become practical through the incrementalism and silo resistance of traditional automakers. Doing the same old thing while expecting different results is, as the saying goes, the definition of insanity. It is time for your company to do better.

We have spent our careers building and evangelizing this path forward. Now it is time for you to pick up the baton and run.

Appendix A: Selected Cybersecurity Guidelines & Standards by Industry

Industry	Standard	Publisher
General Secure System Design & Validation	EU Common Criteria, US FIPS 140, US NIST SP 800 series, ISO 27001, ISO 27002	Various
Auto	SAE J3061; R155/R156; 21434, 26262	SAE; UNECE; ISO
Aviation	DO-326A/B, DO-355A, DO-356A; ARINC Report 667, ARINC Report 835	RTCA, Inc; SAE
Defense/Government	FIPS 140, Common Criteria	US & EU
Energy	IEC 62351,IEC 62443; CIP	IEC; NERC
Finance/Banking	X9 series; Digital Operational Resilience Act	ANSI; EU
Industrial Control	SP800-82	NIST
IoT	NISTIR 8259 series ENISA Baseline Security Recommendations for IoT SB-327	NIST ENISA State of California
Medical/Healthcare	Cybersecurity in Medical Devices: Quality System Considerations and Content of Premarket Submissions – Guidance for Industry and Food and Drug Administration Staff	FDA
Semiconductor	OT Security Guidelines for Semiconductor Device Factories E187-Specification for Cybersecurity for Fab Equipment E188 – Specification for Malware Free Equipment Integration	METI SEMI SEMI

Acknowledgements

The authors wish to thank their friends and colleagues Hank Cohen, Dan Fynaardt, Albert Rooyakkers, and Jimmy Upton for their careful reviews and critiques of the manuscript, which significantly improved its coverage and accuracy.

Bibliography

1. *2025 Minimum Elements for a Software Bill of Materials (SBOM), Public Comment Draft;* CISA, Department of Homeland Security; August 2025.
2. *2025 OT Security Financial Risk Report*; Dragos, Inc. 2025.
3. *Automotive trends in 2025 impacting middle*-market organizations; RSM International Ltd.; February 27, 2025; https://www.rsm.global/insights/automotive-trends-2025-impacting-middle-market-organisations; retrieved December 2025.
4. Boehs, E.; *Everything I Know About the XZ Backdoor*; https://boehs.org/node/everything-i-know-about-the-xz-backdoor; March 29,2024; retrieved December 2025.
5. *CNSSP 15 Use of Public Standards for Secure Information Sharing*; Committee on National Security Systems (CNSS); December 2024.
6. Cybersecurity in Medical Devices: Quality System Considerations and Content of Premarket Submissions, Guidelines for Industry and Food and Drug Administration Staff; FDA; June 27, 2025.
7. *Disrupting the First Reported AI-orchestrated cyber espionage Campaign*; Anthropic; November 2025
8. *ENISA Baseline Security Recommendations for IoT in the context of Critical Information Infrastructures*; ENISA; November 2017.
9. *ENISA Threat Landscape 2025*; European Union Agency for Cybersecurity (ENISA); October 2025
10. Erikson, C.; *npm debug and chalk packages compromised*; Akido Security; https://www.aikido.dev/blog/npm-debug-and-chalk-packages-compromised; retrieved December 2025.
11. Executive Office of the President; *Executive Order 14028, Improving the Nation's Cybersecurity; National Archives and Records Administration*; May 17, 2021.
12. Fagan, M.; Megas, K.; Scarfone, K.; Smith, M.; *NISTIR 8259A IoT Device Cybersecurity Capability Core Baseline*; NIST; May 2020.
13. *FIPS 140-3 Security Requirements for Cryptographic Modules*; Department of Commerce; March 22, 2019.

14. Fireye/Mandiant; *Highly Evasive Attacker Leverages SolarWinds Supply Chain to Compromise Multiple Global Victims with SUNBURST Backdoor*; https://cloud.google.com/blog/topics/threat-intelligence/evasive-attacker-leverages-solarwinds-supply-chain-compromises-with-sunburst-backdoor; December 12, 2020; retrieved December 2025.
15. Heath, L.; *Analysis of the Systemic Security Weaknesses of the U.S. Navy Fleet Broadcasting System, 1967-1974, as Exploited by CWO John Walker;* U.S. Army Command and General Staff College Master's Thesis; 2005.
16. Hughes, J.; Diffie, W.;*The Challenges of IoT, TLS, and Random Number Generators in the Real World*; ACMQueue; May-June 2022
17. https://www.aljazeera.com/news/2009/12/18/us-spy-drone-videos-hacked; retrieved October 2025.
18. https://www.psu.edu/news/campus-life/story/hackers-who-remotely-hijacked-jeep-speak-about-cybersecurity-threats; retrieved October 2025.
19. https://www.rsm.global/insights/automotive-trends-2025-impacting-middle-market-organisations; retrieved October 2025.
20. https://www.theregister.com/2025/07/14/train_brakes_flaw; retrieved October 2025.
21. https://www.wired.com/2015/07/hackers-remotely-kill-jeep-highway; retrieved October 2025.
22. *ISO/IEC 15408, Information security, cybersecurity and privacy protection – Evaluation criteria for IT security*; ISO/IEC; 2022
23. *ISO/IEC 27000, Information technology – Security techniques – Information security management systems – Overview and vocabulary, Second Edition*; ISO/IEC; 2018.
24. Lakshmanan, R.; *Researchers Expose New Intel CPU Flaws Enabling Memory Leaks and Spectre v2 Attacks*; The Hacker News; May 16, 2025.

25. Lautenbach, A.; Islam, M.; *HEAVENS HEAling Vulnerabilities to Enhance Software Security and Safety*; The HEAVENS Consortium; 2016
26. *Mandiant M-Trends 2025 Report*; Google; 2025
27. Moix, A.; Lebedev, K.; Klein, J.; *Threat Intelligence Report: August 2025;* Anthropic; August 2025; https://www.cdn.anthropic.com/b2a76c6f6992465c09a6f2fce282f6c0cea8c200.pdf; Retrieved December 2025.
28. Moody, D; Perlner, R., Regenscheid, A.; Robinson, A., Cooper, D; *Transition to Post-Quantum Cryptography Standards*; NIST Internal Report NIST IR 8547 ipd; NIST; November 2024.
29. *Principles for the Secure Integration of Artificial Intelligence in Operational Technology;* US CISA, NSA et al.*; 3 December 2025.*
30. *J3061 Cybersecurity Guidebook for Cyber-Physical Vehicle Systems*; SAE; 2016
31. *Johnson*, R.; Bennett, D.; Elsabagh, M.*; Uhale Digital Picture Frame Security Assessment*; Quokka; November 2025.
32. Karahasanovic, A; Kleberger, P.; Almgren, M.; *Adapting Threat Modeling Methods for the Automotive Industry*; 15th ESCAR Conference; Berlin 2017.
33. Kohnfelder, L.; Garg, P.; *The Threats to Our Products;* Microsoft; 2009.
34. *Regulation (EU) 2024/2847 of the European Parliament and of the Council as of 23 October 2024 on horizontal cybersecurity requirements for products with digital elements and amending Regulations (EU) no 168/2013 and (EU) No 2019/1020 and Directive (EU) 2020/1828 (Cyber Resilience Act)*; European Union; 2024.
35. *Secure by Demand: Priority Considerations for Operational Technology Owners and Operators when Selecting Digital Products*; CISA, NSA, et al; January 13, 2025.
36. *Secure by Design, Shifting the Balance of Cybersecurity Risk: Principles and Approaches for Secure by Design Software*; CISA, NSA et al; October 2023.

37. *Securing the Software Supply Chain: Recommended Practices for Managing Open-Source Software and Software Bill of Materials*; Enduring Security Framework, ODNI, NSA, CISA, et al.; December 2023.
38. *Securing the Software Supply Chain: Recommended Practices for Software Bill of Materials Consumption*; Enduring Security Framework, ODNI, NSA, CISA, et al.; November 2023
39. Souppaya, M.; Scarone, K.; Dodson, D.; *SP800-218, Secure Software Development Framework (SSDF) Version 1.1*; NIST; February 2022.
40. Swain, B.; *Supply chain attacks are exploiting our assumptions*; The Trail of Bits Blog; https://blog.trailofbits.com/2025/09/24/supply-chain-attacks-are-exploiting-our-assumptions/#implicit-trust; retrieved December 2025.
41. The White House; *NSM-10 National Security Memorandum on Promoting United States Leadership in Quantum Computing While Mitigating Risks to Vulnerable Cryptographic Systems*; May 4, 2022.
42. Thomas, G.; *A Proactive Approach to More Secure Code*; Microsoft MSRC; www.microsoft.com/en-us/msrc/blog.2019/07/a-proactive-approach-to-more-secure-code/; retrieved November 2025.
43. Tidy, J.; *"You'll never need to work again": Criminals offer reporter money to hack BBC*; BBC World Service; 28 September 2025.
44. Valasek, C.; Miller, C.; *Adventures in Automotive Networks and Control Units*; IOActive; 2014
45. Zetter, K.; *Countdown to Zero Day*; Broadway Books; New York; 2014

www.ingramcontent.com/pod-product-compliance
Lightning Source LLC
LaVergne TN
LVHW051128210926
848482LV00001B/18
9781067426651